## DO YOU KNOW?

Who was the first woman to climb Mount Everest?

What woman won her first open pocket billiards championship at the age of thirteen?

Who was the first woman in the world to earn over a million dollars for her ability as an athlete?

What woman introduced tennis to the United States?

Who was the first woman racing driver to qualify for the Indianapolis 500?

Which athlete was nicknamed "Little Miss Poker Face"?

Who is the only woman to be named the patron saint of a sport?

Who was the grandmother who dominated women's bowling for two decades?

What international tennis star appeared in the movie *The Horse Soldiers*?

What woman struck out Ted Williams?

Answers to these questions—and more—will be found in this book.

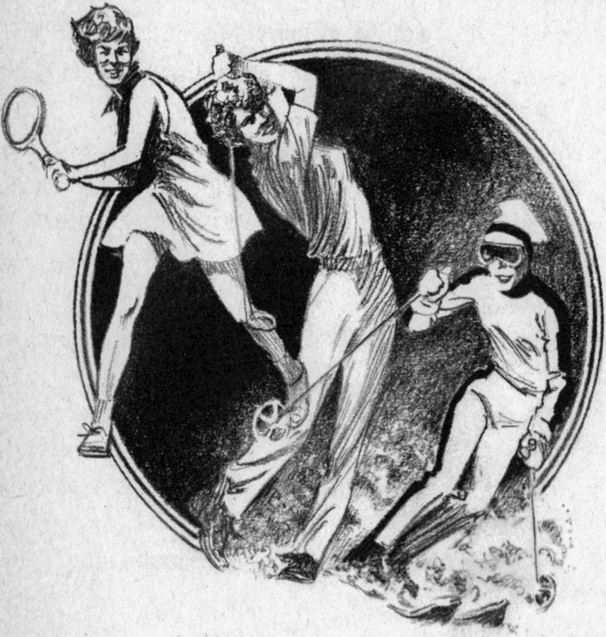

a HANDY BOOK

# WOMEN IN SPORTS
# Records, Stars, Feats, and Facts

LOUIS PHILLIPS and
KAREN MARKOE

Illustrations by Paul Frame

HBJ

Harcourt Brace Jovanovich
New York and London

ST. PHILIPS COLLEGE LIBRARY

Text copyright © 1979 by
Louis Phillips and Karen Markoe
Illustrations copyright © 1979 by Paul Frame

All rights reserved. No part of
this publication may be reproduced or
transmitted in any form or by any means,
electronic or mechanical, including photocopy,
recording, or any information storage and
retrieval system, without permission
in writing from the publisher.

796.092
P561

Requests for permission to make copies of
any part of the work should be mailed to:
Permissions, Harcourt Brace Jovanovich, Inc.,
757 Third Avenue, New York, New York 10017

Printed in the United States of America

LIBRARY OF CONGRESS CATALOGING IN PUBLICATION DATA
Phillips, Louis.
Women in sports.
(A Handy book)
SUMMARY: Contains brief career biographies of
35 women athletes and a summary of women's
achievements in sports.
1. Athletes, Women—Biography—Juvenile literature.
2. Sports for women—Records—Juvenile literature.
[1. Athletes. 2. Sports—Records]
I. Markoe, Karen, joint author.
II. Frame, Paul, 1913–  III. Title.
GV697.A1P45   796'.092'2 [B]   79-87527
ISBN 0-15-299186-7

First edition
B C D E

Dedicated with love to
our sisters,
Leslie Hall and Lorna Kitchens
and
Joan Davidman

## ACKNOWLEDGMENTS

A book of this nature could not have been compiled without the enormous labors of hundreds of statisticians, sports reporters, historians, and compilers of numerous record books and encyclopedias. The authors particularly wish to acknowledge:

W. R. Schroeder, of the Citizens Savings Athletic Foundation

Jim Balukas

Norma Walker, of the Association for Intercollegiate Athletics for Women

Mrs. Karl J. Rustman, of the United States Women's Curling Association

Daniel L. Dorman of the Information Center of the Women's Professional Football League.

*Her inferior strength and sedentary habits confine her within the domestic circle; she is kept aloof from the bustle and storm of active life.*

—THOMAS R. DEW "DISSERTATION ON THE CHARACTERISTIC DIFFERENCES BETWEEN THE SEXES," 1835

# Contents

**How It Used To Be** xvii

**GALLERY OF STARS**

Jean Balukas, Florence Chadwick, Barbara Cochran, Nadia Comaneci, Maureen Connolly, Amelia Earhart, Gertrude Ederle, Chris Evert, Peggy Fleming, Althea Gibson, Janet Guthrie, Dorothy Hamill, Carol Heiss, Sonja Henie, Joan Joyce, Nelli Kim, Billie Jean King, Micki King, Olga Korbut, Marion Ladewig, Lillian Leitzel, Suzanne Lenglen, Nancy Lopez, Helen Wills Moody, Martina Navratilova, Annie Oakley, Mary Jo Peppler, Judy Rankin, Cathy Rigby, Wilma Rudolph, Eleanora Sears, Kathy Whitworth, Mickey Wright, Sheila Young, Babe Zaharias

*pages* 1–71

**RECORDS, FEATS, AND FACTS**

**Archery** 74

   U.S. National Open Freestyle Champions 75
   U.S. National Open Barebow Champions 75

**Auto Racing** 76

| | |
|---|---|
| **Badminton** | 77 |
| U.S. Open Singles Champions | 77 |
| **Baseball** | 78 |
| **Basketball** | 79 |
| **Bowling** | 81 |
| Career Money Winners over $100,000 | 82 |
| Women's International Bowling Congress Champions Since 1970 | 82 |
| All-Time Women's International Bowling Congress Records | 83 |
| U.S. National Singles Duckpin Bowling Champions Since 1970 | 84 |
| **Boxing** | 85 |
| **Bullfighting** | 87 |
| **Canoeing** | 88 |
| Olympic Singles Kayak Champions | 88 |
| **Croquet** | 89 |
| **Curling** | 90 |
| USWCA National Champions | 90 |
| **Cycling** | 91 |
| U.S. National Amateur Bicycling Race Champions Since 1970 | 92 |

## Diving — 93

- Olympic Springboard Champions — 93
- Olympic Platform Champions — 95

## Fencing — 97

- Olympic Foil Champions — 97
- U.S. National Foil Champions — 97

## Football — 99

## Golf — 100

- U.S. Open Champions Since 1970 — 101
- U.S. Amateur Champions Since 1970 — 101
- Ladies Professional Golf Association's Hall of Fame — 102

## Gymnastics — 103

- Gymnastics Coach Par Excellence — 104
- Olympic Champions — 105

## Horse Racing — 106

## Horseshoe Pitching — 107

- U.S. National Champions Since 1970 — 107

## Ice Skating — 108

- U.S. National Outdoor Speed Skating Champions Since 1970 — 109
- Figure Skating — 109

| | |
|---|---:|
| World Figure Skating Champions Since 1970 | 110 |
| Winter Olympic Figure Skating Champions | 111 |
| **Mountain Climbing** | 112 |
| **Power Lifting** | 114 |
| **Roller Skating** | 115 |
| U.S. National Speed Champions Since 1970 | 116 |
| **Shooting** | 117 |
| U.S. National Indoor Rifle Champions Since 1972 | 118 |
| All-Round U.S. National Skeet Shooting Champions Since 1970 | 118 |
| **Skiing** | 119 |
| Alpine World Cup Champions Since 1970 | 119 |
| Winter Olympic Alpine Downhill Champions | 120 |
| Winter Olympic Slalom Champions | 121 |
| **Softball** | 122 |
| U.S. National Major Fast Pitch Champions | 122 |
| U.S. National Major Slow Pitch Champions Since 1970 | 123 |

## Swimming — 124

- Marathon Swimming — 126
- World Record Holders — 127

## Tennis — 129

- British Singles Champions Since 1970 — 131
- U.S. Singles Champions Since 1970 — 131
- French Singles Champions Since 1970 — 132
- Italian Singles Champions Since 1970 — 132
- Australian Singles Champions Since 1970 — 133
- International Tennis Hall of Fame — 134

## Track and Field — 135

- Discus Throw — 135
  - *Olympic Discus Champions* — 136
- Olympic High Jump Champions — 137
- Javelin Throw — 138
  - *Olympic Javelin Champions* — 139
- Olympic Long Jump Champions — 140
  - *U.S. Long Jump Records* — 141
- Running — 142
  - *World Running Records Since 1976* — 144
- Olympic Shot Put Champions — 145

## Volleyball — 146

## Water Skiing — 147

- U.S. National Overall Champions Since 1970 — 148

U.S. National Slalom Champions
   Since 1970     148

**Award Winners**     149

Associated Press Women Athletes
   of the Year     149
James E. Sullivan Memorial
   Trophy Winners     151
World Trophy Winners     152
Black Athletes Hall of Fame     157

**Just for Fun**     158

What the Athletes Said     158
Women Athletes and the Movies     159
Sisters     161
Ah, Sweet Mystery of Youth     163
Age Is No Barrier     165
Who Are the Sports Heroes of
   Young Americans?     167
Off the Record     168
Colorful Nicknames     169
What's Your Olympic IQ?     170
First Ladies     171
Looking Toward the Future     172

# How It Used to Be

It is not surprising that we can point to few great women athletes in the 1800s. In that century, most women believed that they were fragile creatures and that exercise could only injure their delicate bodies. Middle-class and wealthy women particularly were subject to fainting spells, headaches, and nervous disorders.

Of course, there were some "modern" women who believed differently. One of the best known was Catharine Beecher, the sister of Harriet Beecher Stowe, of *Uncle Tom's Cabin* fame. She was the first American woman to publicly encourage physical activity for members of her sex. In her school for girls in Hartford, Connecticut, Catharine Beecher urged women to exercise. Calisthenics became part of the physical education program at her school and was soon added in other girls' schools as well.

Getting women to exercise was not the only problem. Another was to get them to dress in a healthful manner. Their clothing bound them in unnatural ways. Whalebone corsets gave women who could afford to wear them hourglass figures with tiny waists, the fashion of the day. But tight clothing probably made them sick as well.

Gradually, over the decades, some women began to participate in certain sports. Ice skating became popular for both sexes in the 1850s, and croquet in the next decade. For active females, the corseted costume was not practical. Some adopted the Bloomer costume, baggy pants under a loose-fitting smock. However, these women were usually subjected to ridicule.

In the 1880s, bicycling became a popular sport across the country. Long dresses got caught in the spokes of the wheels, so shorter dresses became the accepted fashion.

Just before the turn of the century, many women who had leisure time began to turn to golf and tennis in their free hours. Clothing was simplified to allow them to participate in these sports.

By the turn of the century it was no longer considered unfeminine for women to engage in certain sports for exercise and recreation.

# GALLERY OF STARS

## Jean Balukas

At four, she stood on a box to reach the billiard table.

**Jean Balukas** (1959—) was only four when her parents bought a billiard table for her two older brothers, but she was fascinated with the game even then. She learned by watching her brothers, and she managed to play by standing on a box. □ At the age of nine she entered her first U.S. Open Billiards Championship. Traveling from Brooklyn, New York, to Lansing, Michigan, the schoolgirl began her first championship tournament on a tearful note. Thinking that the child was just playing with the cues, tournament officials told her to stop. Her father had to convince them that she was a contender. She then defeated the Michigan champion and won her first match. At thirteen, she became the U.S. women's champion, a title she won six times in a row. Then, in 1978, she became world champion. She has also won the Women's Pro Billiards Alliance, making her the top contender on the women's pro tour.

## Florence Chadwick

She was the first woman to swim the English Channel both ways.

**Florence Chadwick** (1918—) swam the English Channel in 1950, after thirty-two men and women had already accomplished the feat. Still, the California woman's crossing was something special. For one thing, she set a record for women by completing the swim in just 13 hours, 20 minutes. For another, she followed the France-to-England swim with one from England back to France. With that second swim, she became the first woman in history to make the round trip. □ The England-to-France swim was the harder of the two crossings, since she was swimming against the tides and was bothered by winds and fog. In the early part of the trip, she felt seasick and had to be given pills to ease the queasiness in her stomach. Throughout much of the 16-hour, 22-minute ordeal, she could not see the boat alongside her due to fog, and she was cold because her protective coating of grease had washed away.

## Barbara Cochran

Her best friend and fiercest competitor is her sister.

**Barbara Cochran** (1951—) grew up in a family in which the parents were enthusiastic skiers and the children spent all their spare time on skis. Her father even built a ski lift in the backyard of their home in Richmond, Vermont. ☐ At age thirteen, Barbara beat her older sister, Marilyn, in racing competition. In 1969, sixteen-year-old Barbara, just five-foot-one, and 110 pounds, won the U.S. National Giant Slalom Competition. In 1970, she took second in the World Championships, followed by two World Cup victories. ☐ At Sapporo, Japan, in the 1972 Winter Games, three of the fourteen members of the U.S. Women's team were named Cochran. Only sister Linda, the youngest, did not qualify. Under treacherous conditions, made worse by poor visibility, Barbara won out of a field of forty-two competitors. She brought home the first gold medal won by an American Alpine skier since Andrea Mead Lawrence won two in the 1952 Olympics.

## Nadia Comaneci

She received seven perfect scores in the 1976 Olympics

**Nadia Comaneci** (1961—) was the first gymnast ever to achieve a perfect score of ten. In the 1976 Olympics, held in Montreal, Canada, the fourteen-year-old Romanian girl scored seven perfect tens. No wonder she was voted the world's best female athlete! Nadia Comaneci returned home with three gold medals and a bronze medal. ☐ Winning was nothing new for this extraordinary gymnast. She was only eight years old when she became the junior champion of Romania. That was just two years after Bela Karoly, an outstanding Romanian gymnastic coach, had noticed the little girl playing in a schoolyard. He was astounded by her natural talent and offered to become her coach. ☐ When Nadia Comaneci scored her triumph at Montreal, she stood an inch under five feet and weighed just eighty-six pounds. But to see this tiny teen-ager perform left no one in doubt; she was the best in the world.

**Maureen Connolly**

At nineteen she won the grand slam of world tennis.

**Maureen Connolly** (1934–1969) won the hearts of Americans and tennis lovers everywhere in her brief ten-year career. At the age of fifteen, "Little Mo" won the U.S. women's national junior championship. Two years later she became the U.S. Open singles champion and successfully defended her title in 1952 and 1953. ☐ Mo Connolly reached the pinnacle of her career when she was just nineteen. In a single year she won the grand slam of world tennis: the American, French, English, and Australian titles. ☐ A year later, a tragic horseback riding accident ended the young woman's spectacular tennis career. She married and had two children. ☐ In 1969, a saddened sports world noted the death of thirty-five-year-old Maureen Connolly, the person sports writers had chosen as woman athlete of the year for three straight years, from 1952 to 1954. Cancer had taken the life of this fine young athlete.

## Amelia Earhart

She was the first woman to fly the Atlantic alone.

**Amelia Earhart** (1898–1937?) was called "Lady Lindy," and Americans idolized her. In 1928, she became the first woman to cross the Atlantic Ocean as an airplane passenger. In 1932, she flew the Atlantic solo, the first woman to do so. Charles Lindbergh had made the first trans-Atlantic solo flight in 1927. □ Her parents had always encouraged her to make the most of her talents. When she was learning to fly, she became annoyed with male teachers who objected to her stepping out of her feminine role, as they saw it, so she found women instructors. Her record-breaking fifteen-hour flight showed, she said, "that women can sometimes do things themselves if given the chance." □ Five years after her historic flight, she attempted to fly around the world with co-pilot Frederick J. Noonan. The plane, a Lockheed Electra, developed mechanical difficulties over the Pacific. Nothing was heard from her again.

## Gertrude Ederle

She proved that a woman could swim the English Channel.

**Gertrude Ederle** (1906—) swam the English Channel in 1926, when many still doubted that a woman could swim a distance of twenty-one miles. Not only did the New York City–born swimmer overcome choppy waters to reach Dover, England, from the coast of France in record-breaking time, but she actually had to swim a total of thirty-five miles, due to the harsh sea conditions. When Trudy Ederle returned to the United States, her native city welcomed her with a ticker-tape parade, and she became an overnight heroine. ☐ Two years earlier, at the 1924 Olympic Games held in Paris, she won a gold medal as the U.S. team placed first in the 400-meter relay. She also came home with two bronze medals that year. ☐ Despite her successes, Gertrude Ederle was not to remain in the public eye for long. When she was still in her twenties, her athletic career was short-circuited by a serious back injury. Nevertheless, she continued her life-long interest in sports as a swimming instructor for deaf New York youngsters.

## Chris Evert

She is the 1970s queen of the tennis courts.

**Chris Evert** (1955—), perhaps more than any other tennis player of the 1970s, attracted the notice of fans by her cool precision on the courts. Nearly always composed during a match, she was nicknamed the "Ice Maiden." ☐ She first came to national attention when she reached the quarterfinals of the U.S. Open at Forest Hills in 1971. Although she was defeated by Billie Jean King, fans who saw the Florida teenager play that day had no doubt that she would some day be the best. ☐ In 1974, she captured the Wimbledon title for the first time, and the Associated Press chose her Woman Athlete of the Year. In 1975, she won the U.S. Singles Championship, a title she successfully defended in 1976, 1977, and 1978. In 1977, she earned more than a half million dollars, making her the leading money winner among women tennis players that year.

## Peggy Fleming

At fifteen, she was the top woman figure skater in the United States.

**Peggy Fleming** (1948—) was the only American to win a gold medal in the 1968 Winter Games, held in Grenoble, France. The nineteen-year-old California-born skater was beautiful to behold as she moved to the music with the grace of a ballerina. ☐ Winning was nothing new to the five-foot-three-and-a-half-inch, 106-pound skater. In 1964, she won the U.S. Women's Figure Skating title. Only fifteen years old at the time, she was the youngest woman to hold the title, which she retained until she retired from amateur athletics in 1968. For 1966, 1967, and 1968 she held the World Championship title as well. ☐ Shortly after her Olympic victory, she began to appear on television specials and with the Ice Follies. Millions have watched her dazzling performances on TV and in live appearances since she proudly carried home Olympic gold in 1968.

## Althea Gibson

She showed that prejudice had no place on the tennis courts.

**Althea Gibson** (1927—), no less than Jackie Robinson, showed the sports world that prejudice has no place on the playing field. Born in South Carolina, she grew up in New York City, where she learned to play tennis with the help of the Police Athletic League. Her early victories were in Negro tournaments. In 1948, she became the national Negro woman champion, a position she held for ten years. ☐ In 1950, she became the first black tennis player to compete in the U.S. Open at Forest Hills. The next year she became the first black American to compete at Wimbledon, England. Despite these moral victories, major success on the amateur circuit eluded her until 1957, when she won the women's singles and doubles championships at Wimbledon and repeated her singles triumph at Forest Hills. New York City greeted her with a parade down Fifth Avenue. In 1958, she repeated her victories. Then, having conquered the tennis world, she turned her great strength and drive to golf.

## Janet Guthrie

She raced in the Indy 500, the first woman to enter.

**Janet Guthrie** (1938—) became the first woman to compete in the most prestigious auto race of them all, the Indianapolis 500, on Memorial Day, 1977. This was no mean achievement, considering that women were not even allowed in the pits, where the cars are repaired and refueled, until 1970. □ In 1977, the willowy five-foot-nine-inch, 135-pound driver from Iowa City, Iowa, qualified for the Indy 500 on her second attempt. In her car, the *Lightning*, she was clocked at 191 miles per hour. □ She was raised in Florida, where her father was a pilot, and she learned to fly when she was thirteen. By seventeen Janet Guthrie was a licensed pilot. She is also an experienced parachutist. □ She excels at precision driving, known as "gymkhana," and at endurance driving. Both skills helped her in her first Indy race, when she finished twenty-seven laps and came in twenty-ninth, and in her second, in 1978, when she finished a respectable ninth.

## Dorothy Hamill

She practiced skating seven hours a day for ten years.

**Dorothy Hamill** (1957—) chose sound tracks from old Errol Flynn movies to accompany her four-minute free-style routine in the 1976 Olympic figure skating competition. More important, she practiced seven hours a day, six days a week, eleven months a year, for ten years of her life! The result of such devotion was a gold medal in the 1976 Winter Games, held in Innsbruck, Austria. □ She was already the U.S. titleholder in women's figure skating for three years in a row, beginning in 1974. After her Olympic win, she gave up amateur competition to perform with the Ice Capades. □ The five-foot-three-inch skater, nicknamed "Squint" because she is extremely nearsighted, still maintains a rigorous training schedule. Although she no longer needs to practice seven hours a day, it is not unusual to see her on the ice at five in the morning.

## Carol Heiss

She was a ballerina on ice skates.

**Carol Heiss** (1940—) began to ice-skate at the age of five. She showed talent right from the start, and her parents encouraged her to practice the long, hard hours necessary to become a champion. Her coach, Pierre Brunet, knew she could become the best in the world. In 1956 she did. □ At the age of sixteen, the girl from New York City won the World Women's Figure Skating title, and she maintained her number-one position for five years. However, an Olympic gold medal still eluded her. Another American skater, Tenley Albright, had defeated her earlier in 1956. □ In 1960, in the Winter Games in Squaw Valley, California, she achieved her goal. The five-foot-three-inch, 108-pound athlete exhibited extraordinary technical skill and the grace of a ballerina as she whirled around the ice. She was only the second American woman ever to win an Olympic figure skating competition.

## Sonja Henie

She competed in the Olympics at the age of ten.

**Sonja Henie** (1912–1969) was already the Norwegian women's titleholder when she skated in the 1924 Winter Olympics at the age of twelve. Although she finished last, she retained her Norwegian title for four years while waiting for the next Olympics. ☐ In 1928, the sixteen-year-old from Oslo stunned Olympic audiences in the free-skating event by performing ballet on ice, so different from the stiff, formal skating usually seen in international competition. It won Sonja her first Olympic gold medal. Four years later she won another gold medal, at the Winter Games in Lake Placid, New York. Then, in 1936, she became the first woman skater to win a gold medal for the third consecutive time. ☐ As a pro, she became the first woman athlete to earn more than a million dollars. In fact, she earned more than $50 million from movies and personal appearances. Known as the "Norwegian Doll," the tiny star made figure skating popular the world over.

## Joan Joyce

She once struck out Ted Williams.

**Joan Joyce** (1940—) has the distinction of being the only woman ever to strike out Boston Red Sox slugger Ted Williams. □ As a child, she played baseball with her brother and her father, who was a coach. At thirteen she was good enough to play on a fine women's softball team, the Brakettes of Stratford, Connecticut. At seventeen, called on to relieve the Brakettes' star pitcher, she gave up no hits, and her team won the National Fast Pitch Softball Championship. □ Her amateur pitching over the next seventeen years was equally sensational, and her batting average was better than .400! The five-foot-nine-inch athlete led the Brakettes to national and world titles in 1974, when they became the first American team to win the world championship. □ In the tradition of Eleanora Sears and Babe Didrikson, she is an all-around athlete, at home on a softball field, basketball court, golf course, or bowling alley.

## Nelli Kim

She was the best gymnast on the best gymnastic team in the world.

**Nelli Kim** (1957—) won individual gold medals for the floor exercises and the side horse vault in the 1976 Olympics, held in Montreal, Canada. The Russian girls' team was the best in the world, and she was the best Russian gymnast. ☐ Of course, she worked hard to achieve her world championship. Women gymnasts must compete in four different categories: the floor exercises, the uneven parallel bars, the balance beam, and the side horse vault. From the age of nine, Nelli attended a special gymnastics school where practice sessions lasted five hours a day. ☐ In many sports, being little is a liability; in gymnastics, it is an asset. Nelli Kim, who is part Korean, is small. She moves to the music that accompanies the floor exercises with extraordinary grace. Outgoing and playful, she is always a great favorite with the audience, particularly in the floor exercises. And best of all, she seems to enjoy herself as much as the audience enjoys watching her perform.

## Billie Jean King

Nobody has done more to gain equality for women in sports.

**Billie Jean King** (1943—) learned to play tennis at the age of ten. Her family was devoted to sports, and her brother, Randy Moffet, became a professional baseball player. ☐ Billie Jean practiced hours each day. In 1966, the native Californian defeated Maria Bueno of Brazil to win at Wimbledon. In 1967, she successfully defended her singles title and won the women's doubles and mixed doubles titles as well. She also won the U.S. Open at Forest Hills that summer. She was ranked first in the world in women's amateur tennis. ☐ In 1973, 50 million television viewers saw her beat fifty-five-year-old former Wimbledon champ Bobby Riggs at the Houston Astrodome in three straight sets. She has done more to gain equality for women in sports than anyone else. She organized the Women's Tennis Association because she believed that women players deserved to be well-paid professionals, the same as men.

## Micki King

She broke her arm in one Olympics but returned to win a gold medal in another.

**Micki King** (1944—) was an outstanding diver, and she fully expected to win a medal at the 1968 Olympics. Instead, she broke her arm while attempting an especially difficult dive. Deeply disappointed about her accident, she retired from the sport that she loved. She was twenty-four years old at the time. ☐ But Micki King was not one to stay on the sidelines for long. In the 1972 Olympics, now a captain in the Air Force, she won a gold medal at Munich. Satisfied now that she had the prize that had eluded her four years earlier, she retired from amateur athletics to coach other divers and to encourage sports-minded youngsters to compete in amateur sports. When Captain Micki King was named diving coach for the United States Air Force Academy, she became the first woman to join the academic ranks of a U.S. military academy.

## Olga Korbut

She made a mistake and burst into tears.

**Olga Korbut** (1955—) astounded the crowds at the 1972 Olympics, in Munich, Germany. The petite Russian gymnast was seventeen, but she looked much younger. ☐ She had been training with the extraordinary Russian women's team for many years. They were the best in the world, and she was the most popular member of the team. She looked forward to the 1972 Olympics with great anticipation. But perhaps she tried too hard. She faltered on the uneven parallel bars. Deeply disappointed, she burst into tears. ☐ But she was a real champion. The next day she performed with perfect confidence to win three gold medals and one silver. ☐ In the 1976 Olympics, she was an outstanding competitor, and the crowds were delighted by her exciting performance. She won a silver medal on the balance beam, but the gold went to Nadia Comaneci, and a new star was born.

## Marion Ladewig

She dominated women's bowling for two decades.

**Marion Ladewig** (1915—) is to bowling what Billie Jean King is to tennis or Nadia Comaneci to gymnastics. The five-foot-four-inch blond was named Woman Bowler of the Year for nine years, and when she finally retired in 1965, her career average was a whopping 190! ☐ She won the first Bowling Proprietors Association of America Women's All-Star singles title in 1949, then successfully defended her title in 1950 and again in 1951. Her greatest BPAA win was in 1952, when she had the top average for men and women in the eight-day tournament, an astounding 247.5. ☐ At the age of forty-eight she won the All-Star and the World Invitational. Two years later, the fifty-year-old grandmother, her name indelibly written in the record books, retired from the sport that she had dominated for two decades.

## Lillian Leitzel

She was the star of the Ringling Brothers Barnum and Bailey Circus.

**Lillian Leitzel** (1882–1931) was the star of the Ringling Brothers Barnum and Bailey Circus for her feats as an aerialist. Her twists and flips required great physical strength. Anyone seeing her perform high above the crowds in the circus tent would find it hard to imagine that the tiny woman (she stood just fifty-seven inches high) had the endurance to carry out her astonishing array of tricks on the ropes and rings. ☐ Offstage Lillian Leitzel, whose real name was Lillian Eleanore, had a flair for the dramatic that was rivaled only by her onstage performance. When something did not go her way, she ranted in a variety of languages, including her native German. But she could be the most generous and kind-hearted person, especially with the children of the circus. ☐ In 1931, a faulty ring caused her to fall while performing in Denmark. She did not think her injuries were serious, but two days later she died in a Copenhagen hospital. It was a tragic end to a brilliant circus career.

## Suzanne Lenglen

Was she really sick when she walked off the court in her match against Molla Malloy?

**Suzanne Lenglen** (1899–1938) is the tennis player who many old-timers say was the best woman player of them all. The French woman won the singles title at Wimbledon six times, the Wimbledon doubles six times, and the French singles six times. ☐ Her father taught her accuracy by having her aim at a coin on the far side of the tennis court. ☐ Wherever she played, she brought out the crowds. They were shocked at first when she refused to play in ankle-length dresses, choosing short styles that would not interfere with her play. ☐ She was especially popular in the United States, where fans first saw her play in 1921 at Forest Hills. In a match against Molla Malloy, the defending U.S. champ, Suzanne Lenglen suddenly walked off the court. She said she was sick. But was she? Lenglen was losing at the time, and some claimed that she was just being a poor sport. All the controversy just added to her mystique.

## Nancy Lopez

She is the only player to have been named Golfer of the Year and Rookie Player in the same year.

**Nancy Lopez** (1957—) was awarded the titles of Rookie Player and Golfer of the Year in 1978, the first time in golf history that one athlete received both awards. That same year she entered twenty-five tournaments and won nine of them, including the coveted Ladies Professional Golfers Association title, netting twenty-one-year-old Nancy Lopez a total of $189,813—more than any other woman golfer in 1978. ☐ Born of Mexican-American parents in Roswell, New Mexico, Nancy began to play golf at the age of eight. She was encouraged by her father, who was a fine amateur golfer. ☐ Outgoing and friendly, Nancy Lopez is extremely popular with the fans and the other players. Although she is not very big—she stands five feet, four inches tall—she hits the ball with great strength. Before her career ends, she undoubtedly will set many new golfing records. At twenty-one she was already a golfer to remember.

**Helen Wills Moody**

She dared to play tennis in short dresses.

**Helen Wills Moody** (1905—) was nicknamed "Little Miss Poker Face" by sports writers because of her powers of concentration. She was the outstanding U.S. woman tennis player of the 1920s and 1930s, perhaps the best in the world. ☐ Her achievements were no less than spectacular. She first won the U.S. Open in 1924; the same year she won two gold medals in the Olympics as part of the U.S. tennis team. From 1924 to 1931, she won the U.S. championship a total of six times. In 1927, she became the Wimbledon champion, a position she held eight times, the last in 1938. Added to her credits were doubles and mixed doubles titles, both in the United States and abroad. ☐ When Helen Wills began to compete, women were expected to wear long skirts on the tennis courts and to show their modesty by covering their arms and legs. Helen rebelled and began to appear in more suitable attire. Other women players followed her lead, and soon short tennis outfits for women became accepted.

## Martina Navratilova

She rethought her commitment to the game and emerged a winner.

**Martina Navratilova** (1956—) rivaled Chris Evert for best woman tennis player of 1978. ☐ In 1975, believing that she would have more freedom in the United States, she defected from her native Czechoslovakia. The decision was very difficult, since it meant that she could not return to see her family. ☐ Alone for the first time with a great deal of freedom and a lot of money, she developed bad eating habits and gained thirty pounds. She lost her speed on the court. Nevertheless, she won the women's doubles competition at Wimbledon with Chris Evert in 1976. However, this was followed by a disastrous first-round defeat at the U.S. Open in Forest Hills. ☐ For a time, she stopped playing tennis. She rethought her commitment to the game. She began to diet and to practice regularly. ☐ In 1978, she won her first Wimbledon singles title.

## Annie Oakley

She was the star of Buffalo Bill's Wild West Show.

**Annie Oakley** (1860–1926) was born in a log cabin in 1860, the year Abraham Lincoln was elected president. Her real name was Phoebe Anne Oakley Mozee. As a child, she learned to shoot a rifle, and she supplied her family with much of its food by her skill as a hunter. ☐ At fifteen she won a rifle shooting contest and soon began touring the country in a vaudeville show as a sharpshooter named Annie Oakley. She gained fame by shooting at moving objects while galloping on a horse around a ring. ☐ Her greatest popularity came when she and her husband, Frank Butler, joined Buffalo Bill's Wild West Show. Touring the United States and Europe, the tiny woman sharpshooter was the star of the show. She charmed Queen Victoria, received a medal from the Prince of Wales, and shot ashes from a cigar that Crown Prince Wilhelm (later the German Kaiser) held in his mouth. During World War I, she entertained American soldiers in army camps with her marksmanship.

## Mary Jo Peppler

She was the best volleyball player in the world.

**Mary Jo Peppler** (1944—), the premier volleyball player in the United States, became the first woman superstar in Rotunda, Florida, in 1975. There outstanding women athletes competed in ten events of their own choice, but not in their sport specialty. The six-foot Californian won the softball, basketball, and rowing competitions and excelled in bicycling, swimming, and running. ☐ During her volleyball career, she suffered from being a first-rate player in a team sport that did not receive much attention in the United States. In the 1964 and 1968 Olympics, she could not compensate for the weaknesses of the others on the team. In 1970, she was honored as the best player in the world at the international games in Bulgaria. Only after the 1976 Olympics did Americans begin to train seriously for volleyball. ☐ In 1978, Mary Jo Peppler turned her energies to another sport. At thirty-four, she joined the new women's pro basketball league.

**Judy Rankin**

At seven she scored a hole in one.

**Judy Rankin** (1945—) began to play tennis when she was six. But her father put a golf club in her hand, and the young girl from St. Louis showed a talent for golf that few have equaled. At age seven she scored a hole in one. Judy won two National Pee Wee golf championships, then went on to become one of the top women golfers in the United States. ☐ In 1961, *Sports Illustrated* put her picture on its cover. The editors expected a great future from her, and sixteen-year-old Judy did not disappoint them. By 1977, she had already earned half a million dollars in prize money. The only woman golfer to earn more is Kathy Whitworth. ☐ Although she has won major tournaments all over the world, one eludes her: the U.S. Open, in which the cool, consistent golfer first competed when she was just fourteen. ☐ Judy Rankin shows little emotion on the golf course. In contrast, her husband, Yippy Rankin, walks along with her and openly suffers with every drive and putt.

**Cathy Rigby**

Thousands of girls wanted to be just like her.

**Cathy Rigby** (1952—) made gymnastics a popular sport in this country almost overnight. Thousands of girls wished to be just like her. They wore their hair in pigtails, as she did, and dreamed of winning a medal in Olympic competition. ☐ But Cathy did not win her Olympic medal. In 1972 at Munich, she scored tenth overall. No American gymnast had ever done better. But the star of the show was Olga Korbut, and the medals went to the Russians and Eastern Europeans. ☐ Nevertheless, Cathy Rigby was a winner in international competition in many parts of the world. In 1970, at the World Games in Yugoslavia, she won a silver medal on the balance beam, the first American woman gymnast to do so. Americans began to notice the tiny blond athlete. They rooted for her at Munich, and some of them cried with her when she faltered on the balance beam. ☐ Her prize is knowing that, largely due to her example, American girls now enjoy gymnastics classes. Perhaps one of them will bring home that Olympic medal.

# Wilma Rudolph

As a child she was too sick to walk.

**Wilma Rudolph** (1940—) was a sickly youngster, unable to walk due to the crippling effects of scarlet fever. Yet, in the 1956 Olympics she won a bronze medal for the 400-meter relay, and in 1960 the fleet-footed black college student from Tennessee became the first American woman to win three gold medals in track and field events. She won the 100-meter and 200-meter events, then anchored the 400-meter relay team, which set a world record of 44.4 seconds. ☐ The French called her *La Gazelle,* and the *New York Times* named her one of the ten outstanding women of 1960. The Associated Press chose her as the top female athlete of 1960, and, in 1961, she received the James E. Sullivan Award for the top amateur athlete. ☐ "Skeeter," as she was nicknamed by her high school coach, stood six feet tall and was as graceful as a fawn. She held every American and world record in the 100- and 200-meter dashes, both indoors and out.

## Eleanora Sears

They thought she was unfeminine because she played to win.

**Eleanora Sears** (1881–1968) flew a plane, played polo and golf, raced motorboats, and swam—and she did them all very well. She was born into a wealthy Boston family and a society that did not think it polite for women to participate in strenuous athletics. What particularly incensed the upper class was that the society sportswoman would often wear men's clothing. And she played to win! ☐ In 1928, she was the women's singles champion in squash. In tennis, she was the national doubles champ on four occasions. Where others rode, Eleanora Sears walked. She walked the forty-seven miles from Providence, Rhode Island, to Boston, and the seventy-three miles from Newport to Boston. ☐ If she had to ride, she preferred horses. "Elea," as she was called, raised show horses and race horses. By the time of her death, it had become respectable, even admirable, for women to do what she had always dared to do: devote their energies to athletics.

**Kathy Whitworth**

Golf changed her life.

**Kathy Whitworth** (1935—) was an awkward, chubby teen-ager until she discovered golf. Then her magnificent talent transformed her into a confident, slim young woman and one of the best golfers in the world. ◻ Although she won the first tournament that she entered, the New Mexico State Amateur in 1957, the young Texan soon turned professional and had a rather rocky early career. However, by 1962, her steadiness as a player earned her a respectable $17,000, second only to Mickey Wright, the top player on the Ladies Professional Golf Association Tour. In 1965 and 1966, the Associated Press chose Kathy Whitworth the outstanding Woman Athlete of the Year. ◻ By 1975, her earnings had set a record for women's golf, going well above the half-million-dollar mark. She was number one, the rightful heir of Mickey Wright, since the former champ had retired from the tournament circuit in 1965.

## Mickey Wright

She was named Woman Athlete of the Year two years in a row.

**Mickey Wright** (1935—) is probably the best long-ball hitter in the history of women's golf. Her fascination with golf began in childhood. Babe Didrikson Zaharias was her idol, and she kept scrapbooks of many famous golfers. ☐ She dominated women's golf in the early 1960s. The five-foot-nine-inch, 150-pound athlete once shot a 62 in tournament play, the best round of golf by a woman. In 1961, she won the grand slam of women's golf: the Titleholders, the U.S. Open, and the LPGA. But her best year was 1963, perhaps the best year for any woman in the history of the sport. Her average score was an incredible 72.81. She won her fourth LPGA title, and for the second year in a row she was named Woman Athlete of the Year. ☐ When she retired from the pro tour in 1965 to return to college, she was the undisputed leader among women golfers. Undoubtedly her pictures are in the scrapbooks of aspiring young golfers.

## Sheila Young

She held titles in speed skating and cycling.

**Sheila Young** (1950—) is one of the greatest athletes that ever lived, dominating two sports in the 1970s. At the 1976 Winter Games in Innsbruck, Austria, the Michigan speed skater captured three Olympic medals and became the first American woman to win three individual medals in the Winter Olympic games. That same year, she was the U.S. titleholder in women's cycling and the world sprint cycling champion. ☐ Her parents, both skaters and cyclists, taught Sheila to skate when she was two. At four she was riding a two-wheeled bicycle without training wheels. ☐ In 1973, when she became the first U.S. cyclist to win an international championship in more than a half century, she crashed twice in the course of the race and suffered a deep head wound but nevertheless stayed in the race. The five-foot-four-inch, 130-pound athlete is always in training.

## Babe Zaharias

She was probably the best woman athlete who ever lived.

**Babe Didrikson Zaharias** (1914–1956) wanted to be the best athlete that ever lived. Many believe that she was. An Associated Press poll in 1949 named her the best woman athlete of the twentieth century. She excelled in baseball, basketball, swimming, and tennis, but she won fame in other sports. In the 1932 Olympics, the young Texan won two gold medals, one for the javelin throw, the other for the eighty-meter hurdles. She won a silver medal in the high jump. ☐ A few years later, Mildred Didrikson (nicknamed "Babe" after the great Babe Ruth) began to play golf. Soon she was the best woman golfer in the country. Although she was small, she could drive the ball 300 yards. She won the women's U.S. Open three times. ☐ In 1952, she underwent her first operation for cancer but was back on the golf course just weeks after she left the hospital. The disease took her life in 1956. Her autobiography, *This Life I've Led,* was published a year before her death.

# RECORDS
# FEATS
# AND FACTS

# Archery

In the 1972 Olympics, Doreen Wilbur of the United States won a gold medal in the archery event. Another American, LuAnn Ryon, captured the archery gold medal in 1976.

Who was the greatest woman archer of all time? Certainly Janina Spychajowa-Kurkowaska of Poland would have some claim to the title. She was the world champion archer seven times—in 1931, 1932, 1933, 1934, 1936, 1939, and 1947.

Mrs. M. C. Howell was the U.S. women's archery champion in 1885. She went on to win the championship again in 1886, 1890, 1891, 1893, 1895, 1896, 1898, 1899, 1900, 1902, 1903, 1904, 1905, and 1907. Many consider her to be the greatest U.S. women's archer of all time.

## U.S. NATIONAL OPEN
## FREESTYLE ARCHERY CHAMPIONS

| ARCHER | STATE | YEAR |
| --- | --- | --- |
| Ann Butz | New York | 1970 |
| Darlene Collier | Utah | 1971 |
| Darlene Collier | Utah | 1972 |
| Barbara Morris | Kentucky | 1973 |
| Barbara Morris | Kentucky | 1974 |
| Barbara Morris | Kentucky | 1975 |
| Janet Boatman | New York | 1976 |
| Janet Boatman | New York | 1977 |
| Winnie Eicher | Pennsylvania | 1978 |

## U.S. NATIONAL OPEN
## BAREBOW ARCHERY CHAMPIONS

| ARCHER | STATE | YEAR |
| --- | --- | --- |
| Janie Wright | Texas | 1970 |
| Evvy Briney | California | 1971 |
| Janis Beverly | Georgia | 1972 |
| Janis Beverly | Georgia | 1973 |
| Janis Beverly | Georgia | 1974 |
| Gloria Shelley | Connecticut | 1975 |
| Fronzine Greene | Kansas | 1976 |
| Gloria Shelley | Connecticut | 1977 |
| Rebecca Wallace | Pennsylvania | 1978 |

# Auto Racing

In 1977, Janet Guthrie became the first woman in the world to qualify for the Indianapolis 500. She finished twenty-ninth.

Shirley Muldowney, who bills herself as the fastest woman in drag racing and who is known to racing fans as "Cha Cha," won the National Hot Road Association Nationals in 1976 and 1977.

In 1965, Lee Breedlove, at Bonneville Flats, Utah, set a woman's land speed record by driving a jet-propelled car 335.07 miles per hour over a one-kilometer course.

At England's famous Brookland track, Mrs. E. M. Thomas set the ladies outer-circuit lap record in 1928, when she completed the course in her Bugatti at 120.88 miles per hour. Seven years later, Mrs. Gwenda Stewart lapped the track in a Derby-Miller at 135.95 miles per hour. The first women's auto race in England took place at Brookland in 1908, when Mrs. Locke-King beat out four competitors to win first prize. Mrs. Locke-King's average speed in that 1908 race was 50 miles per hour.

# Badminton

Judy Devlin Hashman, the best women's badminton player in the history of the game, retired from competition in 1967 after winning her tenth world singles title.

Dorothy Walton, badminton champion, voted one of the six outstanding Canadian athletes of the half century, was the Canadian female athlete of the year in 1950, and was named to the Canadian Sports Hall of Fame.

## U.S. OPEN BADMINTON SINGLES CHAMPIONS

| PLAYER | NATION | YEAR |
| --- | --- | --- |
| E. Takenak | Japan | 1970 |
| Norigo Tagai | Japan | 1971 |
| Eva Twedborg | Sweden | 1972 |
| Eva Twedborg | Sweden | 1973 |
| Cindy Baker | United States | 1974 |
| Judianne Kelly | United States | 1975 |
| Gillian Gilks | England | 1976 |
| Pam Bristol | United States | 1977 |
| Cheryl Carton | United States | 1978 |

# Baseball

Who was the first woman to pitch in organized baseball? Credit must be given to Lizzie Stroud. She was hired by Ed Barrow to pitch in the old Atlantic League shortly before the turn of the century.

In 1975, Christine Wren was chosen to work in minor league training camps as an umpire. She was the only woman among fifteen eligible umpires to be selected for the assignment.

In 1931, Babe Didrikson Zaharias tossed a baseball 296 feet to win the Women's Outdoor Baseball Throw.

During an exhibition game, female southpaw Jackie Mitchell struck out Lou Gehrig and Babe Ruth.

# Basketball

It happened on December 9, 1978, in the Milwaukee Arena, the opening game of the Women's Professional Basketball League (WBL). In front of a crowd of 7,824, the Chicago Hustle defeated the Milwaukee Does by a score of 92–87. High scorer in the game, with 30 points, was Debra Woddy Rossow, a 5-foot-10-inch center-forward.

At opening day there were eight teams in the WBL. The Western Division consists of the Does and the Hustle, as well as the Iowa Cornets and the Minnesota Fillies. The Eastern Division teams are the New York Stars, the New Jersey Gems, the Dayton Rockettes, and the Houston Angels.

The tallest player in the league is 6-foot-4-inch Sheila Patterson. The oldest are Karen Logan, player-coach of the Chicago Hustle, and pro volleyball star Mary Jo Peppler, both thirty-four.

The women's game consists of four quarters, each lasting twelve minutes. The ball used in the league is slightly smaller than the one used in the men's league.

Will it be the beginning of a new era in women's professional sports? Only time will tell.

The Wade Trophy is awarded to the outstanding woman basketball player of the year. In 1978, the trophy was awarded to Carol Blazejowski, of Montclair College, in New Jersey. She scored 40 or more points in her last three college games.

Basketball star Anne Meyers, of the University of California at Los Angeles, was selected the 1978 Female College Athlete of the Year by the Association for Intercollegiate Athletics for Women.

In December 1978, Sue Gunter, of Stephen F. Austin State College, was named head coach of the 1980 U.S. Olympic women's basketball team.

Women's basketball got its start in the United States at Smith College in 1892, when Senda Berenson introduced the game to her students. The game had been invented only the year before by James Naismith of Springfield, Massachusetts.

Babe Didrikson, who won renown in golf and track, also played basketball. In the early 1930s, she played for a team called the Golden Cyclones, and at that time Babe was considered to be the greatest woman basketball player in the United States.

# Bowling

In the history of bowling, only one woman has been selected International Bowler of the Year four times: Marion Ladewig, of Grand Rapids, Michigan. She was named Bowler of the Year in 1957, 1958, 1959, and 1963. Shirley Garms, Dorothy Fothergill, Betty Morris, Patty Costello, and Judy Soutar have each won the award twice.

In January 1978, Wendy Jackson set a U.S. record for ten-year-old girls by bowling a 272 game, a game in which she also bowled seven consecutive strikes.

Beverly Otner, of Tucson, Arizona, and Betty Morris, of Stockton, California, have each bowled four perfect games, as sanctioned by the Women's International Bowling Congress.

From 1972 through 1974, the Peanuts team of Hammond, Indiana, set a WIBC record by losing 132 consecutive games.

## CAREER MONEY WINNERS OVER $100,000 (THROUGH 1978)

| PLAYER | AMOUNT |
|---|---|
| Patty Costello, of Union City, California | $120,958 |
| Betty Morris, of Stockton, California | $118,077 |
| Judy Soutar, of Kansas City, Missouri | $104,645 |

## WOMEN'S INTERNATIONAL BOWLING CONGRESS (WIBC) CHAMPIONS SINCE 1970

| SINGLES | YEAR | ALL EVENTS | YEAR |
|---|---|---|---|
| Dorothy Fothergill | 1970 | Dorothy Fothergill | 1970 |
| Ginny Younginer | 1971 | Lorrie Koch | 1971 |
| D. D. Jacobson | 1972 | Mildred Martorella | 1972 |
| Bobby Buffaloe | 1973 | Toni Calvery | 1973 |
| Shirley Garms | 1974 | Judy Soutar | 1974 |
| Barbara Leicht | 1975 | Virginia Park | 1975 |
| Bev Shonk | 1976 | Betty Morris | 1976 |
| Akiko Yamaga | 1977 | Akiko Yamaga | 1977 |
| Mae Bolt | 1978 | Annese Kelly | 1978 |

## ALL-TIME WOMEN'S INTERNATIONAL BOWLING CONGRESS RECORDS

| BOWLER | RECORD AND DATE |
|---|---|
| Georgene Cordes, of Bloomington, Minnesota | 18 consecutive strikes 1970–1971 |
| Joan Taylor, of Syracuse, New York | 27 consecutive spares 1973–1974 |
| Frieda Wood, of Fort Worth, Texas | 147-game marathon, 72 hours, 13 minutes January 30, 1973 |
| Maureen Harris, of Madison, Wisconsin | 1,065-point 4-game series, 1975–1976 |
| Betty Morris, of Stockton, California | 1,564-point 6-game series, 1975–1976 |
| Barbara Thorberg, of Jennings, Missouri | 222 league average 1974–1975 |

## U.S. NATIONAL SINGLES DUCKPIN BOWLING CHAMPIONS SINCE 1970

| BOWLER | SCORE | YEAR |
| --- | --- | --- |
| Martha Venturini | 578 | 1970 |
| Sue Marchone | 460 | 1971 |
| Barbara Brown | 461 | 1972 |
| Agnes Claughsey | 435 | 1973 |
| Lori Cabral | 432 | 1974 |
| Delina Rock | 437 | 1975 |
| Doris Shortt | 467 | 1976 |
| Linda Rosen | 526 | 1977 |
| Doris Gravelin | 493 | 1978 |

# Boxing

Hill's Theater in New York City was the scene of the first U.S. women's boxing match, held on March 16, 1876. Rose Harland was defeated by Nell Saunders. For her labors, Nell Saunders received a silver butter dish.

The first woman in the United States to be granted a license to work as a judge for boxing matches was Carol Polis. She was issued a license by the New York State Athletic Commission in July 1974.

In 1976, a woman's boxing match was held in Virginia City, Nevada. Caroline Svendsen, thirty-four years old, knocked out Jean Lange of Phoenix, Arizona, in fifty seconds of the first round. A thousand spectators were in attendance.

Also in 1976, Gwen Hibbler fought Tyger Trimiarin to a draw. The fight was held in Philadelphia, with about 6,000 in attendance.

Maurice Golesworthy, in his *Encyclopedia of Boxing* (London, 1975) points out that "probably the first woman to gain distinction in the ring was Elizabeth Wilkinson in 1727." He also describes a fight held in the last part of the eighteenth century: "In June 1795 'Gentleman' Jackson seconded Mary Ann Fielding of Whitechapel in 'a well-fought contest' against 'a noted Jewess of Wentworth Road, seconded by Dan Mendoza.' Fielding was declared the winner in 1 hour, 20 minutes, after flooring her opponent 'upwards of 70 times.'"

# Bullfighting

On July 4, 1955, the El Paso *Herald Post* printed the following story about Georgina Knowles, who then held the title of Rojoneadora—Lady Bullfighter on Horseback: "[Georgina Knowles] has made history as the only American girl to fight on horseback.

"She is the first American girl to fight in the plaza in Mexico City, the first to do capework atop a horse, and the first and only fighter to place *banderillas* from horseback with both hands."

One of the first descriptions of lady bullfighters is to be found in Haldeen Broddy's essay "Lady Bullfighters," published in *Password of the El Paso County Historical Society* (Winter, 1963). Mr. Broddy describes Patricia Hayes, who in 1951 played bassoon in the El Paso Symphony and fought bulls in Texas and Mexico: "At Acapulco she received repeated ovations for her strategy, winning plaudits for being the only girl bullfighter to set the *banderillas* (barbed hooks) into her animal's shoulders before making the kill." Patricia Hayes killed fifteen *toros* her first year.

# Canoeing

## OLYMPIC SINGLES KAYAK CHAMPIONS

| WINNER | NATION | YEAR |
| --- | --- | --- |
| K. Hoff | Denmark | 1948 |
| Sylvi Saimo | Finland | 1952 |
| E. Dementieva | U.S.S.R. | 1956 |
| Antonia Seredina | U.S.S.R. | 1960 |
| Ludmila Khvedosiuk | U.S.S.R. | 1964 |
| Ludmila Pinaeva | U.S.S.R. | 1968 |
| Yulia Ryabchinskaya | U.S.S.R. | 1972 |
| Carola Zirzow | East Germany | 1976 |

# Croquet

According to sports historian John Durant, "The game of croquet, which arrived here from England during the Civil War and swept the country like a plague, is unique in the history of American sports. It is the first outdoor game played by women, the first played by both sexes."

In England, the first women's croquet championship was held in 1869 and won by Mrs. Joad.

In 1976, Nelga Young was ranked by the U.S. Croquet Association as the number one woman croquet player in the United States.

# Curling

## USWCA NATIONAL CHAMPIONS

The United States Women's Curling Association (USWCA) sponsors championship matches featuring eight teams in round-robin play. This championship has been in existence for only two years, though the USWCA has sponsored a national Bonspiel since 1949.

| TEAM | PLAYERS | YEAR |
| --- | --- | --- |
| Westchester, New York | Margaret Smith, *Skip*<br>Cynthia Smith<br>Jackie Gant<br>Eve Switzor | 1977 |
| Wausau, Wisconsin | Sandy Robarge, *Skip*<br>Elaine Collins<br>Jo Shannon<br>Virginia Morrison | 1978 |

# Cycling

In December 1977, thirty-five-year-old Joyce Sulanke won the U.S. Cycling Federation National Senior Women's Cyclo-Cross Championships held in Milwaukee, Wisconsin. She cycled 9.5 kilometers in 1 hour, 29 minutes, and 20 seconds.

From August 16 to 27, 1978, the World Championship Cycling events were staged in Munich, West Germany. The world champion in the sprint was Galina Zareva of the Soviet Union.

In August 1978, Esther Salmi, of Chester, Connecticut, cycled 25 miles in 1 hour, 6 minutes, and 4.81 seconds, to win the time trials at Port Washington, Wisconsin.

## U.S. NATIONAL AMATEUR BICYCLING ROAD RACE CHAMPIONS SINCE 1970

| CYCLIST | YEAR |
| --- | --- |
| Audrey McElmury | 1970 |
| Mary Jane Reoch | 1971 |
| Debbie Bradley | 1972 |
| Eileen Brennan | 1973 |
| Jane Robinson | 1974 |
| Linda Stein | 1975 |
| Connie Carpenter | 1976 |
| Connie Carpenter | 1977 |
| Barbara Hintzen | 1978 |

## U.S. NATIONAL AMATEUR BICYCLING SPRINT RACE CHAMPIONS SINCE 1970

| CYCLIST | YEAR |
| --- | --- |
| Sheila Young | 1971 |
| Sue Novarra | 1972 |
| Sheila Young | 1973 |
| Sue Novarra | 1974 |
| Sue Novarra | 1975 |
| Sheila Young | 1976 |
| Sue Novarra | 1977 |
| Sue Novarra | 1978 |

# Diving

## OLYMPIC SPRINGBOARD DIVING CHAMPIONS

| DIVER | POINTS | YEAR |
|---|---|---|
| Aileen Riggin, of the United States | 539.90 | 1920 |
| Elizabeth Becker, of the United States | 474.50 | 1924 |
| Helen Meany, of the United States | 78.62 | 1928 |
| Georgia Coleman, of the United States | 87.52 | 1932 |
| Marjorie Gestring, of the United States | 89.27 | 1936 |
| NO OLYMPICS HELD | | 1940 |
| NO OLYMPICS HELD | | 1944 |
| Victoria M. Draves, of the United States | 108.74 | 1948 |
| Patricia McCormick, of the United States | 147.30 | 1952 |
| Patricia McCormick, of the United States | 142.36 | 1956 |
| Ingrid Kramer, of West Germany | 155.81 | 1960 |
| Ingrid Kramer Engel, of West Germany | 145.00 | 1964 |

| DIVER | POINTS | YEAR |
|---|---|---|
| Sue Gossick, of the United States | 150.77 | 1968 |
| Micki King, of the United States | 450.03 | 1972 |
| Jennifer Chandler, of the United States | 506.19 | 1976 |

# OLYMPIC PLATFORM DIVING CHAMPIONS

| DIVER | POINTS | YEAR |
|---|---|---|
| Greta Johansson, of Sweden | 39.90 | 1912 |
| NO OLYMPICS HELD | | 1916 |
| Stefani Fryland, of Denmark | 34.60 | 1920 |
| Caroline Smith, of the United States | 166.00 | 1924 |
| Elizabeth Pinkston, of the United States | 31.60 | 1928 |
| Dorothy Poynton, of the United States | 40.26 | 1932 |
| Dorothy Poynton Hill, of the United States | 33.92 | 1936 |
| NO OLYMPICS HELD | | 1940 |
| NO OLYMPICS HELD | | 1944 |
| Victoria M. Draves, of the United States | 68.87 | 1948 |
| Patricia McCormick, of the United States | 79.37 | 1952 |
| Patricia McCormick, of the United States | 84.85 | 1956 |
| Ingrid Kramer, of West Germany | 91.28 | 1960 |
| Lesley Bush, of the United States | 99.80 | 1964 |

| DIVER | POINTS | YEAR |
| --- | --- | --- |
| Milena Duchkova, of Czechoslovakia | 109.59 | 1968 |
| Urika Knape, of Sweden | 390.00 | 1972 |
| Elena Vaytsekhovskaia, of the U.S.S.R. | 406.59 | 1976 |

# Fencing

## OLYMPIC FOIL CHAMPIONS

| FENCER | NATION | YEAR |
| --- | --- | --- |
| Ellen Osiier | Denmark | 1924 |
| Helene Mayer | West Germany | 1928 |
| Ellen Preis | Austria | 1932 |
| Ilona Schacherer-Elek | Hungary | 1936 |
| NO OLYMPICS HELD | | 1940 |
| NO OLYMPICS HELD | | 1944 |
| Ilona Schacherer-Elek | Hungary | 1948 |
| Irene Camber | Italy | 1952 |
| Gillian Sheen | Great Britain | 1956 |
| Adelheid Schmid | West Germany | 1960 |
| Ildiko Ujlaki | Hungary | 1964 |
| Elene Novikova | U.S.S.R. | 1968 |
| Antonella Rango Lonzi | Italy | 1972 |
| Ildiko Schwarczenberger | Hungary | 1976 |

# U.S. NATIONAL FOIL CHAMPIONS

| FENCER | YEAR |
|---|---|
| Harriet King | 1970 |
| Harriet King | 1971 |
| Ruth White | 1972 |
| Tanya Adamovich | 1973 |
| Gaye Jacobsen | 1974 |
| Nikki Tomlinson | 1975 |
| Ann O'Donnell | 1976 |
| Sheila Armstrong | 1977 |
| Gay Dasaro | 1978 |

# Football

In 1970, Pat Palinkas became the first woman to play football in an all-male league. She played for the Orlando Panthers of the Atlantic Coast League. Her one job was to hold the football for her husband—Steve Palinkas—a place kicker.

In 1965, the Women's Professional Football League (WPFL) was formed and included teams from Cleveland, Akron, Toledo, Dayton, Bowling Green, Buffalo, Cincinnati, and Pittsburgh. Since that time, other women's football associations have been formed, the most prominent being the National Women's Football League. The NWFL is now divided into three divisions: the Western, the Southern, and the Northern. Among the leading NWFL teams are the Cleveland Brewers, the Columbus Pacesetters, the Middletown Mavericks, the Toledo Troopers, the Dallas–Fort Worth Shamrocks, the Houston Hurricanes, the Lawton Tornadoes, and the Oklahoma City Dolls.

# Golf

Mary Queen of Scots was perhaps the first woman golfer. She played the game at the world's oldest golf course, in St. Andrews, Scotland.

In 1978, *Golf Digest* named Janet Anderson Rookie of the Year. In her first season on the Ladies Professional Golf Association (LPGA) tour, Janet Anderson won $11,959 in prize money.

When Marlene Hagge won the 1952 Sarasota Open tournament, she was only eighteen years old and thus became the youngest tournament winner in LPGA history. Nineteen years later, she shot a 29 for 9 holes to set a new record for LPGA-sanctioned play.

In 1963, Mickey Wright won thirteen LPGA tournaments in a single year.

## U.S. OPEN GOLF CHAMPIONS SINCE 1970

| GOLFER | SCORE | YEAR |
|---|---|---|
| Donna Caponi | 287 | 1970 |
| JoAnne Carner | 288 | 1971 |
| Susie Berning | 299 | 1972 |
| Susie Berning | 290 | 1973 |
| Sandra Haynie | 295 | 1974 |
| Sandra Palmer | 295 | 1975 |
| JoAnne Carner | 292 | 1976 |
| Hollis Stacy | 292 | 1977 |
| Hollis Stacy | 289 | 1978 |

## U.S. AMATEUR GOLF CHAMPIONS SINCE 1970

| GOLFER | YEAR |
|---|---|
| Martha Wilkinson | 1970 |
| Laura Baugh | 1971 |
| Mary Budke | 1972 |
| Carol Semple | 1973 |
| Cynthia Hill | 1974 |
| Beth Daniel | 1975 |
| Donna Horton | 1976 |
| Beth Daniel | 1977 |
| Cathy Sherk | 1978 |

# LADIES PROFESSIONAL GOLF ASSOCIATION'S HALL OF FAME

| GOLFER | YEAR ELECTED |
| --- | --- |
| Patty Berg | 1951 |
| Betty Jameson | 1951 |
| Louise Suggs | 1951 |
| Babe Zaharias | 1951 |
| Betsy Rawls | 1960 |
| Mickey Wright | 1964 |
| Kathy Whitworth | 1975 |
| Sandra Haynie | 1977 |
| Carol Mann | 1977 |

# Gymnastics

One of the brightest stars of the 1968 Olympics in Mexico City was Vera Caslavska. The blond athlete participated in all six gymnastic events. She won the all-around, the uneven parallel bars, the side horse vault, and the floor exercises. In the last she tied with Larisa Petrik, of the U.S.S.R., and they each received a gold medal. That gave her four gold medals. She also won two silver medals, one in the balance beam, the other for being a member of the second-place Czech team. Four years earlier in Tokyo she won three individual gold medals.

The Soviet Union won the gold medal seven times for accumulating the most points in women's gymnastics competition in every Olympics from 1952 through 1976.

When gymnastics was first introduced in the United States about 150 years ago, many young women were attracted to the sport. But modesty was uppermost in their minds. No leotards for them! Practically every inch of their bodies was covered, from neck to ankle.

# GYMNASTICS COACH PAR EXCELLENCE

Perhaps one in a hundred girls who hopes to train in gymnastics with Muriel Grossfeld is accepted into her school in Milford, Connecticut. She is no ordinary coach, and the Grossfeld Gymnastics School is no ordinary gymnastics school. Muriel Grossfeld was the women's national gymnastics champion eighteen times. She competed in the Olympics three times and coached two Olympic women's gymnastics teams. She was a stuntwoman in Hollywood and appeared in several films as a gymnast. To be accepted in Muriel Grossfeld's school, the candidate must possess great determination to excel, a strong back, flexibility, and willingness to be criticized. She has a reputation for being a strict coach, but still hundreds of girls try to get into her school each year. Only a dozen or so are selected. They live at the school, attend a regular school in the area, and are instructed in gymnastics five hours a day. But those dozen, like 1978 world champion Marcia Frederick, know that if Muriel Grossfeld accepts them, they have the makings of a champion.

# 1972 OLYMPIC GYMNASTICS CHAMPIONS

| GYMNAST | NATION | EVENT |
| --- | --- | --- |
| Ludmila Turischeva | U.S.S.R. | all-around |
| Olga Korbut | U.S.S.R. | balance beam |
| Olga Korbut | U.S.S.R. | floor exercises |
| Karen Janz | East Germany | side horse vault |
| Karen Janz | East Germany | uneven parallel bars |
|  | U.S.S.R. | team competition |

# 1976 OLYMPIC GYMNASTICS CHAMPIONS

| GYMNAST | NATION | EVENT |
| --- | --- | --- |
| Nadia Comaneci | Romania | all-around |
| Nadia Comaneci | Romania | balance beam |
| Nelli Kim | U.S.S.R. | floor exercise |
| Nelli Kim | U.S.S.R. | side horse vault |
| Nadia Comaneci | Romania | uneven parallel bars |
|  | U.S.S.R. | team competion |

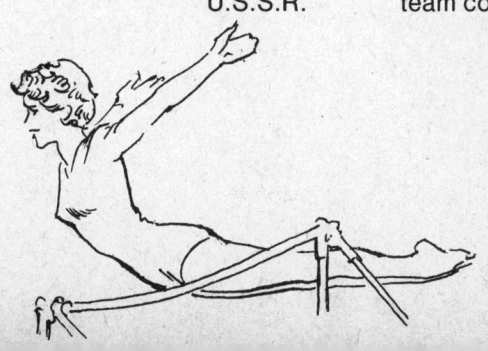

# Horse Racing

The first jockey ever to win the Argentine quadruple crown in one year was Marina Lezcano. The twenty-one-year-old Argentinian won the two-year-old Derby, the Jockey Club Grand Prix, the National Grand Prix, and the Pellegrini—all in 1978.

The first woman to ride in the Kentucky Derby was Diane Crump. Aboard Fathom, she finished fifteenth in the 1970 Derby.

One of the most successful harness racing drivers in the United States is Bea Farber, who usually races her horses on Michigan tracks. By 1978, she had run forty horses in under two minutes. Farber attributes her success to the love she bestows upon her horses. She talks to them and kisses them, in great displays of affection.

# Horseshoe Pitching

Who is the best woman horseshoe pitcher in the world today? The title is presently held by Opal Reno, of Lucasville, Ohio. In the summer of 1978, the world championships were held in Des Moines, Iowa, and Opal Reno won eleven matches without a defeat, beating Lorraine Thomas and Debby Michaud. She threw ringers 82.8 percent of the time. In the Girl's Horseshoe Championship, Linda Pateneaude, of Maine, took top honors.

## U.S. NATIONAL HORSESHOE PITCHING CHAMPIONS SINCE 1970

| PLAYER | PERCENTAGE OF RINGERS TOSSED | YEAR |
| --- | --- | --- |
| Ruth Hangen | 72.0 | 1970 |
| Ruth Hangen | 73.4 | 1971 |
| Ruth Hangen | 76.6 | 1972 |
| Ruth Hangen | 79.6 | 1973 |
| Lorraine Thomas | 80.2 | 1974 |
| Vicki Winston | 73.5 | 1975 |
| Ruth Hangen | 75.6 | 1976 |
| Debbie Michaud | 75.0 | 1977 |
| Opal Reno | 82.8 | 1978 |

# Ice Skating

The only person to become a patron saint of a sport was a Dutch woman named Lidwina. According to the story, in 1396, Lidwina, then a young girl, went ice skating with some friends. A fall on the ice caused a broken rib. While Lidwina was recovering in bed, she became ill with a disease that lasted the rest of her life. It was said that she performed miracles and had visions of a religious nature. The Catholic Church honored her and in 1944 named her the patron saint of skating.

On March 11, 1975, Titiana Averina, of the Soviet Union, set world skating records for 500 and 1,500 meters. Competing in Moscow, she skated the 500-meter distance in 41.7 seconds, beating the old mark of 41.8, held by Sheila Young, of Detroit. Titiana Averina covered the 1,500-meter distance in 2 minutes and 9.9 seconds.

The Winter Olympic games began in 1924, but it wasn't until 1964 that an athlete won four gold medals during a single meet. The athlete was twenty-four-year-old Lidiya Skoblikova, of the Soviet Union. She won gold medals in the 500-, 1,000-, 1,500-, and 3,000-meter events. She covered the 500 meters in 45 seconds flat.

## U.S. NATIONAL OUTDOOR SPEED SKATING CHAMPIONS SINCE 1970

| SKATER | YEAR |
| --- | --- |
| Sheila Young | 1970 |
| Sheila Young | 1971 |
| Nancy Thorne | 1972 |
| Ruth Moore | 1972 |
| Nancy Class | 1973 |
| Kris Garbe | 1974 |
| Nancy Swider | 1975 |
| Connie Carpenter | 1976 |
| Liz Crowe | 1977 |
| Paula Class | 1978 |
| Betsy Davis | 1978 |

## FIGURE SKATING

From 1956 through 1960, Carol Heiss, of the United States, held the world figure skating championship.

At ten years of age, Barbara Ann Scott won the Canadian Junior Skating Championship—the youngest person ever to hold that title (1939). In the 1948 Olympics, she was named ladies figure skating champion. In both 1948 and 1949, Scott was the world champion figure skater. Later, she went on the stage and appeared in the musical *Rose Marie* in London.

# WORLD FIGURE SKATING CHAMPIONS SINCE 1970

| SKATER | NATION | YEAR |
|---|---|---|
| Gabriele Seyfert | East Germany | 1970 |
| Beatrix Schuba | Austria | 1971 |
| Beatrix Schuba | Austria | 1972 |
| Karen Magnusson | Canada | 1973 |
| Christine Errath | East Germany | 1974 |
| Dianne de Leeuw | Netherlands | 1975 |
| Dorothy Hamill | United States | 1976 |
| Linda Fratianne | United States | 1977 |
| Anett Poetzsch | East Germany | 1978 |

# WINTER OLYMPIC FIGURE SKATING CHAMPIONS

| SKATER | NATION | YEAR |
|---|---|---|
| Madge Syers | England | 1908 |
| NO OLYMPICS HELD | | 1912 |
| NO OLYMPICS HELD | | 1916 |
| Magda Mauroy | Sweden | 1920 |
| Herma Szabo-Planck | Austria | 1924 |
| Sonja Henie | Norway | 1928 |
| Sonja Henie | Norway | 1932 |
| Sonja Henie | Norway | 1936 |
| NO OLYMPICS HELD | | 1940 |
| NO OLYMPICS HELD | | 1944 |
| Barbara Ann Scott | Canada | 1948 |
| Jeannette Altwegg | England | 1952 |
| Tenley Albright | United States | 1956 |
| Carol Heiss | United States | 1960 |
| Sjouke Dijkstra | Netherlands | 1964 |
| Peggy Fleming | United States | 1968 |
| Beatrix Schuba | Austria | 1972 |
| Dorothy Hamill | United States | 1976 |

# Mountain Climbing

In September 1978, the first expedition consisting only of women (and their male Sherpa guides) began to climb Annapurna, the tenth-highest mountaintop in the world. Led by Arlene Blum, a biochemist from the University of California, the nine women, along with their six guides, braved avalanches, ice walls, and snowstorms for more than seven weeks. Finally, on October 15, two members of the party, Irene Miller, a forty-two-year-old physicist, and Vera Komarkova, a thirty-five-year-old plant ecologist, reached the summit. They had climbed 26,504 feet! Two Sherpa guides were with them. The climbers placed flags of the United States and Nepal on the top of the mountain along with a banner that read, "A woman's place is at the top."

Two days later two British members of the team, Vera Watson and Alison Chadwick, set out for the summit. But tragically they lost their footing on an ice wall and plunged 2,000 feet to their death.

At the base camp the names of the two dead mountain climbers were inscribed on a rock, added to nine others whose lives were lost in an attempt to conquer Annapurna.

Arlene Blum's team was the fourteenth to attempt to scale the treacherous Himalayan peak but only the fifth to reach the top.

The first woman to climb Mount Kilimanjaro, in Africa, was an Englishwoman, Gertrude Benham, who accomplished the feat in 1909.

The first woman to set foot on the peak of Mount Everest—the world's highest mountain—was Junko Tabei, of Japan. She accomplished the feat on May 17, 1975.

On October 26, 1978, thirty-one-year-old Beverly Johnson, of Kelly, Wyoming, became the first woman to climb El Capitan (located in Yosemite National Park, California) alone. It took her ten days to scale the 3,600 feet of sheer granite.

On May 27, 1975, Phan Thog, a Chinese Tibetan mountain climber, became the second woman to scale Mount Everest.

# Power Lifting

The first woman to lift 1,000 pounds or more in three power lifts was Jan Todd, who weighs less than 200 pounds. In 1977 she bench-pressed 176¼ pounds, dead-lifted 441 pounds, and lifted 424¼ pounds from a squat, for a total of 1,041½ pounds.

In 1895, Josephine Blatt, an American, used a hip and harness lift to lift 3,564 pounds.

# Roller Skating

In 1976, Donna Kiker of Decatur, Georgia, was the United States ladies figure roller skating champion. Jean O'Laughlin, of Waltham, Massachusetts, took the title the following year. In 1978, Patti Marshalewski, of Concordville, Pennsylvania, became the new titleholder.

Natalie Dunn, of Bakersfield, California, has won the world roller skating championship three times—in 1976 when the competition was held in Rome, Italy; in 1977 in Montreal, Canada; and in 1978 in Lisbon, Portugal. Natalie started skating when she was only two years old and won her first regional competition in the Tiny Tot Division (for children seven years old and under) when she was seven years old.

# U.S. NATIONAL SPEED ROLLER SKATING CHAMPIONS SINCE 1970

| SKATER | YEAR |
| --- | --- |
| Colleen Giacomo | 1970 |
| Colleen Giacomo | 1971 |
| April Allen | 1972 |
| Natalie Dunn | 1973 |
| Robin Wilcock | 1974 |
| Marcia Yager | 1975 |
| Marcia Yager | 1976 |
| Marcia Yager | 1977 |
| Linda Dorso | 1978 |

# Shooting

In 1950, Joan Pflueger won the Grand American trapshoot competition at Vandalia, Ohio. She was the only woman to compete, and she defeated men from every state in the union and from Cuba. In winning, the eighteen-year-old woman from Florida broke 100 straight clay pigeons. It was the first time in the fifty-one-year history of the event that a woman was victorious.

In one rifle exhibition, Annie Oakley shot at 5,000 pennies tossed into the air in rapid succession. She hit 4,777 of them.

In August 1977, PFC Mary Stidworthy, of Prescott, Arizona, became the second woman in history to win the National Rifleman's Association's small-bore prone rifle championship. The competition was held at Camp Perry, Ohio, and Mary Stidworthy scored 6,397 points out of a possible 6,400, beating 500 of the best sharpshooters in the country for the title.

Betty Swarthout was the United States high-power rifle champion in 1972, 1974, and 1975.

## U.S. NATIONAL INDOOR RIFLE CHAMPIONS SINCE 1972

| CHAMPION | SCORE | YEAR |
| --- | --- | --- |
| Margaret T. Murdoch | 795 | 1972 |
| Tricia Foster | 796 | 1973 |
| Karen E. Monez | 798 | 1974 |
| Karen E. Monez | 797 | 1975 |
| Karen E. Monez | 800 | 1976 |
| Elaine S. Proffitt | 798 | 1977 |
| Karen E. Monez | 798 | 1978 |

## ALL-ROUND U.S. NATIONAL SKEET SHOOTING CHAMPIONS SINCE 1970

| CHAMPION | SCORE OUT OF 550 TARGETS | YEAR |
| --- | --- | --- |
| Karla Roberts | 535 | 1970 |
| Karla Roberts | 536* | 1971 |
| Claudia Butler | 542 | 1972 |
| Karla Roberts | 545 | 1973 |
| Karla Roberts | 542 | 1974 |
| Jackie Ramsey | 540 | 1975 |
| Valerie Johnson | 539 | 1976 |
| Connie Place | 544* | 1977 |
| Ila Hill | 543 | 1978 |

* 555 targets

# Skiing

In the 1972 Olympics, Marie-Therese Nadig won a gold medal in the downhill event and then won a second gold medal in the giant slalom. She was the first woman ever to win two Olympic gold medals in these events.

Because Israel is a desert country, it is not noted for turning out great skiers. Nevertheless, Israel will be represented in international competition. How? Penny Spiesman, of Kingston, New York, constitutes Israel's one-woman ski team.

## ALPINE WORLD CUP SKIING CHAMPIONS SINCE 1970

| SKIER | NATION | YEAR |
| --- | --- | --- |
| Michel Jacot | France | 1970 |
| Annemarie Proell | Austria | 1971 |
| Annemarie Proell | Austria | 1972 |
| Annemarie Proell | Austria | 1973 |
| Annemarie Proell | Austria | 1974 |
| Annemarie Proell | Austria | 1975 |
| Rosi Mittermaier | West Germany | 1976 |
| Lise-Marie Morerod | Switzerland | 1977 |
| Hanni Wenzel | Liechtenstein | 1978 |

# WINTER OLYMPIC ALPINE DOWNHILL SKIING CHAMPIONS

| SKIER | TIME | YEAR |
|---|---|---|
| Hedi Schlunegger, of Switzerland | 2:28.3 | 1948 |
| Trude Jochum-Beiser, of Austria | 1:47.1 | 1952 |
| Madeleine Berthod, of Switzerland | 1:40.1 | 1956 |
| Heide Biebl, of West Germany | 1:37.6 | 1960 |
| Christl Haas, of Austria | 1:55.39 | 1964 |
| Olga Pall, of Austria | 1:40.87 | 1968 |
| Marie-Therese Nadig, of Switzerland | 1:36.68 | 1972 |
| Rosi Mittermaier, of West Germany | 1:46.16 | 1976 |

# WINTER OLYMPIC SLALOM CHAMPIONS

| SKIER | TIME | YEAR |
| --- | --- | --- |
| Gretchen Fraser, of the United States | 1:57.2 | 1948 |
| Andrea Mead Lawrence, of the United States | 2:10.6 | 1952 |
| Renee Colliard, of Switzerland | 112.3 points | 1956 |
| Anne Heggtveigt, of Canada | 1:49.6 | 1960 |
| Christine Goitschel, of France | 1:35.11 | 1964 |
| Marielle Goitschel, of France | 1:25.86 | 1968 |
| Barbara Cochran, of the United States | 1:31.24 | 1972 |
| Rosi Mittermaier, of West Germany | 1:30.54 | 1976 |

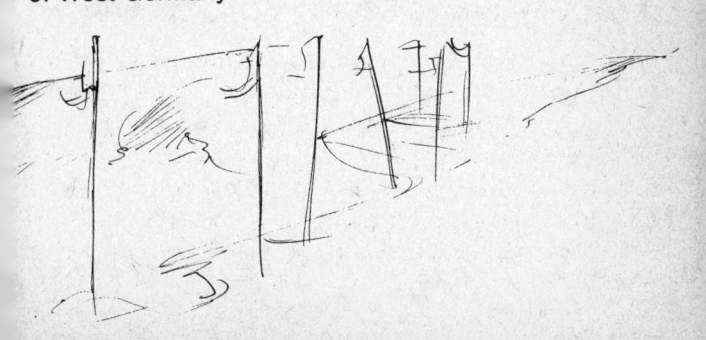

# Softball

In 1933, the first women's softball tournament was held, and the national championship was won by the Great Northerns, of Chicago.

In 1945, Betty Evans Grayson, of Portland, Oregon, pitched 115 consecutive scoreless innings. In her lifetime, she pitched 51 no-hitters and hurled 3 perfect games.

Amy Peralta, of the Phoenix Ramblers, was a star softball pitcher who tossed 300 career shutouts and 50 no-hitters. She was voted into the Amateur Softball Association Hall of Fame.

## U.S. NATIONAL MAJOR FAST PITCH CHAMPIONS

What is the best women's softball team in the United States? Without a doubt, the answer to that question would have to be the Raybestos Brakettes, who hail from Stratford, Connecticut. In 1970, the Orange Lionettes from Orange, California, won the National Women's Major Fast Pitch Championship. But the Raybestos Brakettes have won every single championship from 1971 through 1978.

# U.S. NATIONAL MAJOR SLOW PITCH CHAMPIONS SINCE 1970

| TEAM | YEAR |
| --- | --- |
| Rutenschroer Floral, of Cincinnati, Ohio | 1970 |
| Gators, of Ft. Lauderdale, Florida | 1971 |
| Riverside Ford, of Cincinnati, Ohio | 1972 |
| Sweeney Chevrolet, of Cincinnati, Ohio | 1973 |
| Marks Brothers, North Miami Dots, of Miami, Florida | 1974 |
| Marks Brothers, North Miami Dots, of Miami, Florida | 1975 |
| Sorrento's Pizza, of Cincinnati, Ohio | 1976 |
| Fox Valley Lassies, of St. Charles, Illinois | 1977 |
| Bob Hoffman's Dots, of Miami, Florida | 1978 |

# Swimming

Annette Kellerman was the first woman to wear a one-piece bathing suit. She appeared on Revere Beach in Boston in 1907. Dressed in a one-piece bathing suit, she was promptly arrested. In addition, Kellerman was the first woman to attempt to swim the English Channel. Although she did not succeed, she inspired other women to follow. Annette Kellerman's life story was made into a movie, *Million Dollar Mermaid*, starring Esther Williams.

Sybil Bauer, who died of cancer at the age of twenty-two, was the first woman to break an existing men's world swimming record, when she won the Olympic backstroke event in 1924. At one time, Sybil Bauer held all existing backstroke records for women.

In 1932, Helene Madison, of Seattle, Washington, became the first woman to swim 100 yards in 1 minute flat.

From 1936 through 1942, Ragnhild Hveger, of Denmark, set forty-three world swimming records.

On August 11, 1965, Karen Muir competed in the British Swimming Championships and set a world record in the backstroke, swimming 110 yards in 8.7 seconds. She was all of twelve years old at the time—the youngest person in history to hold a world's record in swimming.

# MARATHON SWIMMING

The greatest marathon swimmer in the world today is without a doubt Diana Nyad. In 1975, she became the first person in the world to swim across Lake Ontario, covering the 32-mile distance in 20 hours. She also holds the record for swimming around Manhattan, covering the 28 miles in 7 hours and 57 minutes.

In 1931, Myrtle Huddleston, of New York City, set an endurance record by remaining afloat in a swimming pool for 87 hours and 27 minutes.

Greta Andersen, who won a gold medal in the 1948 Olympics for the 100-meter sprint, swam 25 miles around Atlantic City, New Jersey, in 10 hours and 17 minutes (1956). Greta Andersen also holds the record for swimming the English Channel more than any other woman—she swam it five times. At one time she held the speed records for crossing the Channel, swimming from France to England in 11 hours and 1 minute, and swimming from England to France in 13 hours and 10 minutes. Greta Andersen's records have since been broken by Cindy Nichols, of Canada, who in 1975 swam the English Channel *nonstop* in 19 hours and 55 minutes.

## SWIMMING WORLD RECORD HOLDERS

| SWIMMER/EVENT | TIME | DATE |
| --- | --- | --- |
| Tracey Wickham<br>1,500-meter freestyle | 16:14.93 | Feb. 2, 1978 |
| Tracey Wickham<br>800-meter freestyle | 8:24.62 | Aug. 6, 1978 |
| Tracey Wickham<br>400-meter freestyle | 4:06.28 | Aug. 24, 1978 |

| SWIMMER/EVENT | TIME | DATE |
| --- | --- | --- |
| Cynthia Woodhead<br>200-meter freestyle | 1:58.53 | Aug. 22, 1978 |
| Barbara Krause<br>100-meter freestyle | 0:55.41 | July 5, 1978 |
| Linda Jezek<br>200-meter backstroke | 2:11.93 | Aug. 24, 1978 |
| Ulrike Richter<br>100-meter backstroke | 1:01.51 | June 5, 1976 |
| Lina Kachushite<br>200-meter breaststroke | 2:31.42 | Aug. 24, 1978 |
| Julia Bogdanova<br>100-meter breaststroke | 1:10.31 | Aug. 22, 1978 |
| Andrea Pollack<br>200-meter butterfly | 2:09.87 | July 4, 1978 |
| Tracy Caulkins<br>200-meter butterfly | 2:09.87 | Aug. 26, 1978 |
| Andrea Pollack<br>100-meter butterfly | 0:59.46 | July 3, 1978 |
| Tracy Caulkins<br>400-meter medley | 4:40.83 | Aug. 24, 1978 |
| Tracy Caulkins<br>200-meter medley | 2:14.07 | Aug. 20, 1978 |

# Tennis

The first woman tennis champion of record is Jean Margot, who played an early version of the game in France in 1427. During her day, she was hailed as "the Joan of Arc" of tennis.

On the other side of the Channel, at Wimbledon, women entered tennis tournaments for the first time in 1884. (Men had been playing at Wimbledon starting in 1877.) A woman known as M. Watson won in 1884. In 1887, Charlotte Dod won the Wimbledon Championship. At the time she was only fifteen years old, the youngest person ever to win at Wimbledon.

Mary Outerbridge introduced tennis to the United States. She first saw the sport played in Bermuda and convinced friends on Staten Island to play the game. Ellen Hansell and Bertha Washington were America's first two women champions. Ellen Hansell won the U.S. Singles Championship in 1887, and Bertha Washington won it the following two years.

The U.S. Tennis Association has ranked Chris Evert the number one U.S. women's player from 1974 through 1978. Not since Alice Marble was ranked number one from 1936 to 1940 has the same woman been in the top position for five consecutive years. In 1978, the top ten were: Chris Evert, Billie Jean King, Tracy Austin, Rosemary Casals, Pam Shriver, Marita Redondo, Kathy May, Anne Smith, Joanne Russell, and Jeanne DuVall.

Playing in the Forest Hills tournament in 1930, May Sutton Bundy (who was the first American woman to win at Wimbledon, in 1904, and in 1907 won it again) slipped on the court and fractured her left leg. Instead of conceding the match, she made use of a crutch and finished the set.

To win the grand slam of tennis, a player must win the singles championships of the United States, Great Britain, France, and Australia—in a single year. Only two women players have ever done it. Maureen Connolly, of the United States, won the grand slam in 1953, and Margaret Court, of Australia, did it in 1970.

In 1978, Pam Shriver was named Rookie of the Year by *Tennis Digest* magazine for her fine performance in the U.S. Open Tennis Championship. At sixteen, she managed to reach the finals.

On November 25, 1978, in Tokyo, fifteen-year-old Tracy Austin upset Wimbledon champion Martina Navratilova 6-1, 6-1, to capture the $20,000 first prize.

## BRITISH SINGLES TENNIS CHAMPIONS SINCE 1970

| PLAYER | YEAR |
| --- | --- |
| Margaret Court | 1970 |
| Evonne Goolagong | 1971 |
| Billie Jean King | 1972 |
| Billie Jean King | 1973 |
| Chris Evert | 1974 |
| Billie Jean King | 1975 |
| Chris Evert | 1976 |
| Virginia Wade | 1977 |
| Martina Navratilova | 1978 |

## U.S. SINGLES TENNIS CHAMPIONS SINCE 1970

| PLAYER | YEAR |
| --- | --- |
| Margaret Smith Court | 1970 |
| Billie Jean King | 1971 |
| Billie Jean King | 1972 |
| Margaret Smith Court | 1973 |
| Billie Jean King | 1974 |
| Chris Evert | 1975 |
| Chris Evert | 1976 |
| Chris Evert | 1977 |
| Chris Evert | 1978 |

## FRENCH SINGLES TENNIS CHAMPIONS SINCE 1970

| PLAYER | YEAR |
| --- | --- |
| Margaret Smith Court | 1970 |
| Evonne Goolagong | 1971 |
| Billie Jean King | 1972 |
| Margaret Smith Court | 1973 |
| Chris Evert | 1974 |
| Chris Evert | 1975 |
| Sue Barker | 1976 |
| Mima Jausovec | 1977 |
| Virginia Ruzici | 1978 |

## ITALIAN SINGLES TENNIS CHAMPIONS SINCE 1970

| PLAYER | YEAR |
| --- | --- |
| Billie Jean King | 1970 |
| Virginia Wade | 1971 |
| Linda Tuero | 1972 |
| Evonne Goolagong | 1973 |
| Chris Evert | 1974 |
| Chris Evert | 1975 |
| Mima Jausovec | 1976 |
| Janet Newberry | 1977 |
| Regina Marsikova | 1978 |

# AUSTRALIAN WOMEN'S SINGLES CHAMPIONS SINCE 1970

| PLAYER | YEAR |
| --- | --- |
| Margaret Smith Court | 1970 |
| Margaret Smith Court | 1971 |
| Virginia Wade | 1972 |
| Margaret Smith Court | 1973 |
| Evonne Goolagong | 1974 |
| Evonne Goolagong | 1975 |
| Evonne Goolagong | 1976 |
| Kerry Reid | 1977 |
| Evonne Goolagong | 1978 |

# INTERNATIONAL TENNIS HALL OF FAME

- May Sutton Bundy
- Mary K. Browne
- Hazel Hotchkiss Wightman
- Molla Bjurstedt Mallory
- Maud Barger Wallach
- Helen Wills Roark
- Helen H. Jacobs
- Sarah P. Danzig
- Alice Marble
- Pauline B. Addie
- Ellen Ford Hansell
- Bertha T. Toumlin
- Juliette Atkinson
- Ellen C. Roosevelt
- Betty N. Shoemaker
- Suzanne Lenglen
- Margaret O. du Pont
- Louise B. Clapp
- Maureen Connolly Brinker
- Eleanora Sears
- Marie Wagner
- Doris Hart
- Shirley F. Irvin
- Althea Gibson Darben
- Elisabeth H. Moore
- Elizabeth Ryan
- Darlene Hard
- Jean Borota
- Mabel Cahill
- Maria E. Bueno
- Kathleen M. Godfree

# Track and Field

The most gold medals won by a woman in Olympic competition is four. In 1948, Fanny Blankers-Koen, of the Netherlands, won gold medals in the 100-meter dash, 200-meter run, 80-meter hurdles, and the 4-×-100-meter relay. In 1964, Betty Cuthbert of Australia won the 100-meter dash, 200-meter run, 400-meter run, and the 4-×-100-meter relay.

## DISCUS THROW

Jan Svendsen was the first American-born woman to throw the discus more than 180 feet. She accomplished the feat in 1976, when she threw the discus 180 feet, 11 inches.

On June 10, 1977, Lynne Winbigler, of Westwood, California, threw the discus 187 feet, 2 inches, to set a new record for American women. The current world record is 232 feet, set by Evelin Jahl, of East Germany, in East Berlin on August 12, 1978.

Only three American women have thrown the discus 180 feet or more: Jan Svendsen, Lynne Winbigler, and Olga Connolly. In 1972, Olga Connolly threw it 187 feet.

## OLYMPIC DISCUS CHAMPIONS

| CHAMPION | DISTANCE | YEAR |
|---|---|---|
| Helena Konopacka, of Poland | 129' 11⅞" | 1928 |
| Lillian Copeland, of the United States | 133' 2" | 1932 |
| Gisela Mauermayer, of West Germany | 156' 3 3/16" | 1936 |
| NO OLYMPICS HELD | | 1940 |
| NO OLYMPICS HELD | | 1944 |
| Micheline Ostermeyer, of France | 137' 6½" | 1948 |
| Nina Romaschkova, of the U.S.S.R. | 168' 8½" | 1952 |
| Olga Fikotova, of Czechoslovakia | 176' 1½" | 1956 |
| Nina Ponomareva, of the U.S.S.R. | 180' 8¼" | 1960 |
| Tamara Press, of the U.S.S.R. | 187' 10½" | 1964 |
| Lia Manolin, of Romania | 191' 2½" | 1968 |
| Faina Melnik, of the U.S.S.R. | 218' 7" | 1972 |
| Evelin Schlaak, of East Germany | 226' 4½" | 1976 |

## OLYMPIC HIGH JUMP CHAMPIONS

| JUMPER | HEIGHT CLEARED | YEAR |
|---|---|---|
| Ethel Catherwood, of Canada | 5' 3" | 1928 |
| Jean Shiley, of the United States | 5' 5¼" | 1932 |
| Ioblya Csak, of Hungary | 5' 3" | 1936 |
| NO OLYMPICS HELD | | 1940 |
| NO OLYMPICS HELD | | 1944 |
| Alice Coachman, of the United States | 5' 6⅛" | 1948 |
| Ester Brand, of South Africa | 5' 5¾" | 1952 |
| Mildred L. McDaniel, of the United States | 5' 9¼" | 1956 |
| Yolanda Balas, of Romania | 6' ¾" | 1960 |
| Yolanda Balas, of Romania | 6' 2¾" | 1964 |
| Miloslava Rezkova, of Czechoslovakia | 5' 11¾" | 1968 |
| Ulrike Meyfarth, of West Germany | 6' 3½" | 1972 |
| Rosemarie Ackermann, of East Germany | 6' 3 9/10" | 1976 |

## JAVELIN THROW

Only three American women have ever thrown the javelin over 200 feet. They are: Kate Schmidt, 227' 5" in 1977; Sherry Calvert, 207' 11" in 1978; and Karin Smith, 203' 10" in 1976.

Only one American woman has ever won an Olympic gold medal in the javelin throw, and that was Babe Didrikson in 1932.

# OLYMPIC JAVELIN CHAMPIONS

| CHAMPION | DISTANCE | YEAR |
|---|---|---|
| Mildred Didrikson, of the United States | 143' 4" | 1932 |
| Tilly Fleischer, of West Germany | 148' 2¾" | 1936 |
| NO OLYMPICS HELD | | 1940 |
| NO OLYMPICS HELD | | 1944 |
| Herma Bauma, of Austria | 149' 6" | 1948 |
| Dana Zatopek, of Czechoslovakia | 165' 7" | 1952 |
| Inessa Janzeme, of the U.S.S.R. | 176' 8" | 1956 |
| Elvira Ozolina, of the U.S.S.R. | 183' 8" | 1960 |
| Mihaela Penes, of Romania | 198' 7½" | 1964 |
| Angela Nemeth, of Hungary | 198' | 1968 |
| Ruth Fuchs, of East Germany | 209' 7" | 1972 |
| Ruth Fuchs, of East Germany | 216' 4" | 1976 |

## OLYMPIC LONG JUMP CHAMPIONS

| JUMPER | DISTANCE | YEAR |
| --- | --- | --- |
| Olga Gyamati, of Hungary | 18' 8¼" | 1948 |
| Yvette Williams, of New Zealand | 20' 5¾" | 1952 |
| E. Kreskinska, of Poland | 20' 9¾" | 1956 |
| Vyera Krepina, of the U.S.S.R. | 20' 10¾" | 1960 |
| Mary Rand, of England | 22' 2¼" | 1964 |
| V. Viscopoleanu, of Romania | 22' 4½" | 1968 |
| Heidemarie Rosendahl, of West Germany | 22' 3" | 1972 |
| Angela Voigt, of East Germany | 22' 2½" | 1976 |

## U.S. LONG JUMP RECORDS

| JUMPER | DISTANCE | YEAR |
| --- | --- | --- |
| Jodi Anderson | 22' 7½" | 1978 |
| Kathy McMillan | 22' 3" | 1976 |
| Sharon Walker | 21' 7½" | 1976 |
| Martha Watson | 21' 7" | 1973 |
| Willye White | 21' 6" | 1964 |

# RUNNING

On January 21, 1979, Ursula Hook, of West Germany, became the first woman to run an indoor 800-meter race in less than 2 minutes. She ran the 800 meters in 1 minute and 59.9 seconds.

Micki Gorman, who once ran 100 miles in 21 hours, held the women's world record in the marathon in 1974. She has been quoted as saying, "If women are strong enough to have babies, they are strong enough to run marathons."

In 1966, Roberta Gibb Bingay became the first woman to compete in the all-male (at that time) Boston Marathon. Running with a hood, she was undetected until she crossed the finish line. The blond runner ran ahead of most of the field of 415 starters. In 1978, 200 women competed in the 26.2-mile Boston Marathon.

In 1979, Joan Benoit, a twenty-one-year-old college student from Cape Elizabeth, Maine, ran the Boston Marathon in two hours, thirty-five minutes, fifteen seconds (2:35.15), a record for a woman. Only two women in the world have posted faster records in marathon competition.

The top two women runners in the 1978 New York City

Marathon were Grete Waitz, who finished in 2 hours, 32 minutes, and 30 seconds (thus setting a new world record for women marathoners), and Marty Cooksey, who finished the 26.2-mile course in 2 hours, 41 minutes, and 55 seconds.

# WORLD RUNNING RECORDS SINCE 1976

| RUNNER | EVENT | TIME | YEAR |
|---|---|---|---|
| Lea Olafsson, of Denmark | 10,000 meters | 31:45.4 | 1978 |
| Lea Olafsson, of Denmark | 5,000 meters | 15:08.8 | 1978 |
| Lyudmila Bragina, of the U.S.S.R. | 3,000 meters | 3:27.1 | 1976 |
| Natalia Maracescu, of Romania | 1 mile | 4:23.8 | 1977 |
| Tatyana Kazankina, of the U.S.S.R. | 1,500 meters | 3:56 | 1976 |
| Tatyana Kazankina, of the U.S.S.R. | 800 meters | 1:54.9 | 1976 |
| Marita Koch, of East Germany | 400 meters | 0:48.94 | 1978 |
| Marita Koch, of East Germany | 200 meters | 0:22.06 | 1978 |
| Marlies Oelsner, of East Germany | 100 meters | 0:10.88 | 1977 |

## OLYMPIC SHOT PUT CHAMPIONS

| CHAMPION | DISTANCE | YEAR |
|---|---|---|
| Micheline Ostermeyer, of France | 45' 1½" | 1948 |
| Galina Zybina, of the U.S.S.R. | 50' 1½" | 1952 |
| Tamara Tishkyevich, of the U.S.S.R. | 54' 5" | 1956 |
| Tamara Press, of the U.S.S.R. | 56' 9⅞" | 1960 |
| Tamara Press, of the U.S.S.R. | 59' 6" | 1964 |
| Margita Gummel, of East Germany | 64' 4" | 1968 |
| Nadezhda Chizhova, of the U.S.S.R. | 69' | 1972 |
| Ivanka Christova, of Bulgaria | 69' 5" | 1976 |

No American woman has ever won an Olympic gold medal in the shot put.

# Volleyball

At the first regional training center ever set up by the U.S. Olympic Committee, twenty American women live and work together in Colorado Springs to improve their volleyball skills. They are hoping to be good enough by 1980 to win an Olympic medal.

Women who have been elected to the Volleyball Hall of Fame include: Lou Sara Clark McWilliams, Jean K. Gaertner, Carolyn Gregory Conrad, Lois Ellen Haraughty, Linda Murphy, Zoann Neff, and Nancy Owen.

# Water Skiing

At age thirteen, Kris Carroll was named 1977s Outstanding female Eastern Water Skier.

In 1939, the first national water-skiing championships were held in Long Island, New York. The first women's all-around champion was Esther Yates.

Not only has Liz Allan-Shetter dominated the U.S. National Water Skiing Championships in this decade, but in 1975, she also won the Overall World Championship by scoring a sensational 4,296 points.

## U.S. NATIONAL OVERALL WATER SKIING CHAMPIONS SINCE 1970

| SKIER | SCORE | YEAR |
| --- | --- | --- |
| Liz Allan | 2,999 | 1970 |
| Liz Allan-Shetter | 2,980 | 1971 |
| Liz Allan-Shetter | 2,878 | 1972 |
| Liz Allan-Shetter | 3,701 | 1973 |
| Liz Allan-Shetter | 2,975 | 1974 |
| Liz Allan-Shetter | 2,647 | 1975 |
| Cindy Todd | 2,876 | 1976 |
| Camille Duvall | 3,075 | 1977 |
| Deena Brush | 3,021 | 1978 |

## U.S. NATIONAL SLALOM WATER SKIING CHAMPIONS SINCE 1970

| SKIER | SCORE | YEAR |
| --- | --- | --- |
| Liz Allan | 49½ buoys | 1970 |
| Christy Weir | 51 buoys | 1971 |
| Christy Weir | 59 buoys | 1972 |
| Liz Allan-Shetter | 57 buoys | 1973 |
| Liz Allan-Shetter | 53 buoys | 1974 |
| Cindy Todd | 56 buoys | 1975 |
| Barbara Cleveland | 51½ buoys | 1976 |
| Cathy Marlow | 51½ buoys | 1977 |
| Deena Brush | 56 buoys | 1978 |

# Award Winners

## ASSOCIATED PRESS WOMEN ATHLETES OF THE YEAR

| ATHLETE | SPORT | YEAR |
|---|---|---|
| Virginia Van Wie | Golf | 1934 |
| Helen Wills Moody | Tennis | 1935 |
| Helen Stephens | Track | 1936 |
| Katherine Rawls | Swimming | 1937 |
| Patty Berg | Golf | 1938 |
| Alice Marble | Tennis | 1939 |
| Alice Marble | Tennis | 1940 |
| Betty Hicks Newell | Golf | 1941 |
| Gloria Callen | Swimming | 1942 |
| Patty Berg | Golf | 1943 |
| Ann Curtis | Swimming | 1944 |
| Babe Didrikson Zaharias | Golf | 1945 |
| Babe Didrikson Zaharias | Golf | 1946 |
| Babe Didrikson Zaharias | Golf | 1947 |
| Fanny Blankers-Koen | Track | 1948 |
| Marlene Bauer | Golf | 1949 |
| Babe Didrikson Zaharias | Golf | 1950 |
| Maureen Connolly | Tennis | 1951 |
| Maureen Connolly | Tennis | 1952 |

| ATHLETE | SPORT | YEAR |
| --- | --- | --- |
| Maureen Connolly | Tennis | 1953 |
| Babe Didrikson Zaharias | Golf | 1954 |
| Patty Berg | Golf | 1955 |
| Patricia McCormick | Diving | 1956 |
| Althea Gibson | Tennis | 1957 |
| Althea Gibson | Tennis | 1958 |
| Maria Bueno | Tennis | 1959 |
| Wilma Rudolph | Track | 1960 |
| Wilma Rudolph | Track | 1961 |
| Dawn Frazer | Swimming | 1962 |
| Mickey Wright | Golf | 1963 |
| Mickey Wright | Golf | 1964 |
| Kathy Whitworth | Golf | 1965 |
| Kathy Whitworth | Golf | 1966 |
| Billie Jean King | Tennis | 1967 |
| Peggy Fleming | Ice Skating | 1968 |
| Debbie Meyer | Swimming | 1969 |
| Chi Cheng | Track | 1970 |
| Evonne Goolagong | Tennis | 1971 |
| Olga Korbut | Gymnastics | 1972 |
| Billie Jean King | Tennis | 1973 |
| Chris Evert | Tennis | 1974 |
| Chris Evert | Tennis | 1975 |
| Nadia Comaneci | Gymnastics | 1976 |
| Chris Evert | Tennis | 1977 |
| Nancy Lopez | Golf | 1978 |

# JAMES E. SULLIVAN MEMORIAL TROPHY WINNERS

| ATHLETE | SPORT | YEAR |
|---|---|---|
| Ann Curtis | Swimming | 1944 |
| Patricia McCormick | Diving | 1956 |
| Wilma Rudolph | Track | 1961 |
| Debbie Meyer | Swimming | 1968 |
| Tracy Caulkins | Swimming | 1978 |

The Sullivan Memorial Trophy is awarded each year by the Amateur Athletic Union to the athlete who, "by his or her performance, example, and influence as an amateur, has done the most during the year to advance the cause of sportsmanship." Since its inception in 1930, over forty male athletes and only five women have received the award.

# WORLD TROPHY WINNERS

Each year the Citizens Savings Athletic Foundation (originally the Helms Athletic Foundation) grants awards to the foremost amateur athletes in six areas of the world—Africa, Asia, Australasia, Europe, North America, and South America-Caribbean. Following are the female recipients of the coveted awards known as the World Trophy.

## Africa

| ATHLETE | SPORT | YEAR |
| --- | --- | --- |
| E. L. Heine, of South Africa | Tennis | 1929 |
| Joan Harrison, of South Africa | Swimming | 1952 |
| Sandra Reynolds, of South Africa | Tennis | 1959 |
| Karen Muir, of South Africa | Swimming | 1966 |

## Asia

| ATHLETE | SPORT | YEAR |
| --- | --- | --- |
| Chi Cheng, of Formosa | Track and Field | 1969 |

## Australasia

| ATHLETE | SPORT | YEAR |
|---|---|---|
| Fanny Durack, of Australia | Swimming | 1915 |
| Marjorie Jackson, of Australia | Track and Field | 1952 |
| Shirley S. de la Hunty, of Australia | Track and Field | 1955 |
| Lorraine Crapp, of Australia | Swimming | 1956 |
| Dawn Frazer, of Australia | Swimming | 1961 |
| Betty Cuthbert, of Australia | Track and Field | 1964 |
| Judy Pollock, of Australia | Track and Field | 1967 |
| Pamela Kilborn, of Australia | Track and Field | 1969 |
| Shane Gould, of Australia | Swimming | 1971 |
| Gail Neall, of Australia | Swimming | 1972 |
| Jenny Turrall, of Australia | Swimming | 1974 |

## Europe

| ATHLETE | SPORT | YEAR |
|---|---|---|
| Lambert Chambers, of England | Golf | 1914 |
| Suzanne Lenglen, of France | Tennis | 1923 |
| Joyce Wethered, of England | Golf | 1925 |
| Sonja Henie, of Norway | Figure Skating | 1936 |
| Ragnhild Hveger, of Denmark | Swimming | 1938 |
| Fanny Blankers-Koen, of the Netherlands | Track and Field | 1948 |
| Tamara Press, of the U.S.S.R. | Track and Field | 1963 |
| Liesel Westermann, of West Germany | Track and Field | 1967 |
| Liese Prokop, of Austria | Track and Field | 1969 |
| Irena Szewinska, of Poland | Track and Field | 1974 |
| Ludmila Turischeva, of the U.S.S.R. | Gymnastics | 1975 |

## North America

| ATHLETE | SPORT | YEAR |
|---|---|---|
| Juliette P. Atkinson, of the United States | Tennis | 1898 |

| ATHLETE | SPORT | YEAR |
|---|---|---|
| Mary Sutton, of the United States | Tennis | 1905 |
| Hazel Hotchkiss, of the United States | Tennis | 1911 |
| Molla Bjurstedt, of the United States | Tennis | 1917 |
| Helen Wills, of the United States | Tennis | 1929 |
| Glenna Collett, of the United States | Golf | 1930 |
| Helene Madison, of the United States | Swimming | 1931 |
| Alice Marble, of the United States | Tennis | 1939 |
| Ann Curtis, of the United States | Swimming | 1944 |
| Pauline Betz, of the United States | Tennis | 1946 |
| Patricia McCormick, of the United States | Diving | 1955 |
| Wilma Rudolph, of the United States | Track and Field | 1960 |
| Keena Rothhammer, of the United States | Swimming | 1973 |
| Shirley Babashoff, of the United States | Swimming | 1975 |

## South America–Caribbean

| ATHLETE | SPORT | YEAR |
|---|---|---|
| Anita Lizana, of Chile | Tennis | 1937 |
| Maria Lenk, of Brazil | Swimming | 1942 |
| Elisabeth Muller, of Brazil | Track and Field | 1945 |
| Maria Bueno, of Brazil | Tennis | 1959 |
| Olga de Angulo, of Colombia | Swimming | 1970 |

# BLACK ATHLETES HALL OF FAME

Althea Gibson
Alice Coachman
Wilma Rudolph
Willye White

# Just for Fun

## WHAT THE ATHLETES SAID

"Swimming is the best sport in the world for women. When a girl indulges in basketball, tennis, or golf, she is all tired at the close of the game. But after a girl has had a good swim, she feels relaxed, cool, her muscles are in order, and her whole make-up, both physical and mental, is at rest and at peace with the world."

—Ethelda Bleibtrey, first U.S.
Women's Olympic swimming champion

"If you see a tennis player who looks as if he is working very hard, then that means he isn't very good."

—Helen Wills Moody

"You know football isn't as difficult a game to play as tennis."

—Alice Marble

## WOMEN ATHLETES AND THE MOVIES

One of the first great women athletes to appear in movies was swimming star Annette Kellerman. In 1914, she starred in *Neptune's Daughters*. In 1916, she made *Daughter of the Gods*.

Tennis star Althea Gibson appeared in *The Horse Soldiers*.

"I . . . have a contract with Columbia Pictures. They want to do a movie about my life. . . . It will show a positive role model of a woman in sports, for a change. In the Babe Didrikson movie, she got cancer and died, and in *The Other Side of the Mountain*, the skier got paralyzed. They make it seem like only bad things happen to women athletes."

—Suzy Chaffee, 1978

Babe Didrikson Zaharias, Betty Hicks, Alice Marble, and Gussie Moran can all be seen in the Spencer Tracy–Katharine Hepburn film *Pat and Mike* (1952).

Esther Williams made her screen debut in 1943 in *Andy Hardy's Double Life*.

The woman athlete who scored the biggest success in Hollywood was probably Sonja Henie, who appeared in *One in a Million*, *Thin Ice*, *Happy Landing*, *My Lucky Star*, and many others. When she made her screen debut in 1937, the *New York Times* film critic wrote: "Being neither sports writer nor poet, this department finds it hard to cloak in adequate language an occasion of such historic importance as the screen debut of Miss Sonja Henie, the figure skating queen. . . . Satisfactorily blonde, dimpled, and ingratiating, when her magical skates are removed, she becomes (as possibly everybody knows by this time) a combination of Freya, Yseult, and La Belle Dame Sans Merci."

## SISTERS

The Devlin sisters, Susan Devlin Peard and Judy Devlin Hashman, teamed up to win the English doubles crown in badminton in 1954, 1956, and 1960.

Marilyn, Barbara, and Linda Cochran made the Cochrans the first family of skiing in the 1960s and 1970s. When they entered a race, the only question was which Cochran would win.

When Chris Evert ceases to dominate women's tennis, will her place be taken by sister Jeanne, or perhaps the baby of the family, sister Clare?

Traci and Terri Nelson are twin sisters who happen to be champion skiers. Terri is the ninth-ranked downhill skier in the United States, and Traci is ranked seventh. In addition, they have a twenty-three-year-old sister named Cindy, who is the U.S. ski team's number-one downhill racer.

Sharon Firth and Shirley Firth, of Canada, both excelled at cross-country skiing. Shirley won the Canadian Senior 5 KM Championship five times, and Sharon won the 5 KM in 1975 and finished second in 1971.

Margaret Curtis and Harriet Curtis, of Boston, were both golf stars in the first decade of the twentieth century. Harriet won the Women's Golf Championship in 1906, while her sister was champion in 1907, 1911, and 1912.

## AH, SWEET MYSTERY OF YOUTH

In 1972, when Jean Balukas won the U.S. Women's Open Pocket Billiards Championship, she was all of thirteen years old.

In 1977, tennis star Tracy Austin became the youngest person to take part in the Virginia Slims Tour. Sporting pigtails, Tracy was fourteen years old at the time, and she brought her schoolwork on the tour with her.

In 1975, at the age of fourteen, Mwing Mwanjala was the only woman from her nation to be selected for the Tanzanian long-distance team. She had run 1,500 meters in 4 minutes and 34.6 seconds to set a Tanzanian record.

Jane Marie (Peaches) Bartkowicz won the Junior Wimbledon Tennis Championship at age fifteen—the youngest player ever to win that event. In fact, from age eleven until she turned eighteen, she never lost a tennis match to anyone in her age group.

Skiing star Suzy Chaffee learned to ski at the age of two and a half.

At age seventeen, Debbie Polk set a Texas state basketball record for high school girls when she scored 68 points in a single game.

## AGE IS NO BARRIER

Marathon runner Micki Gorman posted her fastest records when she was in her forties.

Zaddie Bunker received her pilot's license on her sixty-fifth birthday. She learned to fly a plane the year before.

On May 18, 1973, Josephine Borges, of Oakland, California, bowled a perfect game. At age fifty-seven, she was the oldest person ever to bowl a 300 game in Women's International Bowling Congress–sanctioned play.

At forty-eight, Marion Ladewig won the two most important individual bowling tournaments, the All-Star and the World Invitational.

Forty-four-year-old Eleanora Sears won the National Women's Singles Championship in squash.

Doris Coburn, a grandmother from Buffalo, New York, was a big money winner on the pro bowling circuit in 1978. She will not reveal her age.

Hazel Hotchkiss Wightman, the winner of forty-five national tennis titles, won her last one when she was sixty-eight years old!

In the grueling sport of offshore power boat racing, the world titleholder and 1978 U.S. champion is Betty Cook, a fifty-five-year-old grandmother from Newport Beach, California. Speeds sometimes reach 95 miles an hour, and the crew is blinded by the sun and the spray from the salt water, making power boat racing one of the most dangerous of all sports.

# WHO ARE THE SPORTS HEROES OF YOUNG AMERICANS?

According to a 1977 Gallup Youth Survey, boys and girls in the United States included three women in their top ten choices:

| | |
|---|---|
| Chris Evert | number 2 |
| Nadia Comaneci | number 5 |
| Billie Jean King | number 6 |

The results were somewhat different when only the girls' choices were tabulated:

| | |
|---|---|
| Chris Evert | number 1 |
| Nadia Comaneci | number 2 |
| Billie Jean King | number 4 |
| Olga Korbut | number 10 |

While girls selected men and women as their favorites, boys selected men only.

Who are your sports heroes?

## OFF THE RECORD

Quick. Can you name the woman in this book who has had a rose named in her honor? The answer is Amelia Earhart, the Amelia Earhart rose.

The only U.S. athlete whose "Frozen Face of Fame"—a wax representation—is on display at the internationally famous Madame Tussaud's Wax Museum in London is track star Wilma Rudolph.

The first woman Olympic torchbearer was Norma Enriqueta Basilio. In the games held in Mexico City in 1968, she carried the torch to light the flame that burned in Olympic stadium.

## COLORFUL NICKNAMES

| | |
|---|---|
| *The Pearl* | Debbie Mason |
| *Little Miss Sure Shot* | Annie Oakley |
| *Little Mo* | Maureen Connolly |
| *Lady Lindy* | Amelia Earhart |
| *Cha Cha* | Shirley Muldowney |
| *Little Miss Poker Face* | Helen Wills Moody |
| *Mighty Mouse* | Elaine Tanner |
| *The Norwegian Doll* | Sonja Henie |
| *Squint* | Dorothy Hamill |
| *Skeeter* | Wilma Rudolph |

# WHAT'S YOUR OLYMPIC IQ?

Give yourself one point for each correct answer. Three right: You're a bronze medalist. Four right: You're a silver medalist. Five right: Congratulations! You've won the gold.

1. In the 1976 Olympics, she had seven perfect scores of 10 in gymnastic competition. Who is she?

2. In the 1932 Olympics, she was disappointed that she could enter only three events, although she qualified in eight. Who is she?

3. Nicknamed the "Norwegian Doll," this figure skater won her first Olympic medal in 1928 at the age of sixteen. Who is she?

4. In the 1964 Olympics held in Tokyo, three American women, Dawn Frazer, Sharon Stouder, and Kathy Ellis placed first, second, and third. What was their sport?

5. She was the only American to win a gold medal in the 1968 Winter Olympics. Her sport is skating. Who is she?

ANSWERS:
1. Nadia Comaneci
2. Babe Didrikson Zaharias
3. Sonja Henie
4. Swimming. They won their medals for the 100-meter freestyle.
5. Peggy Fleming

## FIRST LADIES

Can you match each name with the event that made her a famous first?

1. Diane Crump
2. Gertrude Ederle
3. Billie Jean King
4. Ann Curtis
5. Wilma Rudolph

A. First woman to swim the English Channel.
B. First woman professional athlete to win over $100,000 in a season.
C. First black woman to win the Sullivan Trophy.
D. First woman jockey in the Kentucky Derby.
E. First woman to win the Sullivan Trophy.

ANSWERS: 1-D, 2-A, 3-B, 4-E, 5-C.

## LOOKING TOWARD THE FUTURE

In 1978, fifteen-year-old Marcia Frederick, of Springfield, Massachusetts, opened a new chapter in U.S. women's gymnastics. She became the first American woman gold medal winner in international competition. Her victory came on the uneven bars at the world gymnastics championship held in Strasbourg, France.

Judges gave the young gymnast 9:95 points out of a possible 10 for being the first gymnast to perform a complicated routine called the "Stalder Shoot" on the uneven bars.

Winning the gold medal took exceptional talent and a lot of hard work. Marcia Frederick practices five hours a day at the special gymnastics school that she attends in Milford, Connecticut.

In a field traditionally dominated by the Soviet Union and Eastern European countries, Marcia Frederick has proven that American women gymnasts can compete successfully. She and many other aspiring young American women gymnasts are looking forward to Olympic competition.

Pam Shriver is a tennis player to watch. In 1978, at the U.S. Open, held in the spanking-new National Tennis Center in Flushing Meadow, New York, the sixteen-year-old high school student stunned the tennis world by defeating Martina Navratilova, the world's top-ranked woman tennis player. Although the lanky young star lost to Chris Evert in the finals, she became the youngest woman player ever to reach the finals of the U.S. Open.

The mild-mannered gal from Lutherville, Maryland, is a fierce competitor, with her tremendous serve and overhead smash. Sports writers also note that she is a modest winner and a good loser. She should be an inspiration to aspiring tennis players and to all young athletes.

The 1980 Olympics will be held in Moscow, and Leslie Russo plans to be there. She is a young gymnast from Durham, Connecticut, and already she has astounded audiences in many parts of the world. In 1978, in Japan, fourteen-year-old Leslie performed an extraordinary feat, two back somersaults in which she landed on her feet. It is called a "doubleback."

Back in the United States, Leslie Russo continued her triumph. In gymnastics competition held in Philadelphia, she placed first in all four gymnastic events: the uneven parallel bars, the side horse vault, the balance beam, and the floor exercises.

On the road again, she won gold medals in Spain and South Africa. It seemed as if Leslie Russo could not be stopped. But she was, at least temporarily, due to back problems, tonsillitis, and other physical ailments. She thinks she can overcome them, and she hopes that there is an Olympic medal in her future. People who have seen Leslie Russo perform will not be the least bit surprised.

In 1978, Andrea Jaeger was only thirteen years old. But she already held seven national tennis titles. Her most important wins were the girls national sixteen-and-under clay court singles and the doubles, with her sixteen-year-old sister, Suzy.

Andrea Jaeger, an A student in junior high school in Lincolnshire, Illinois, does not look like a magnificent tennis player. She weighs just seventy-six pounds and stands an inch under five feet.

Still, many people who watch young tennis stars say Andrea is the girl to watch. Her doubles partner used to be Tracy Austin, already a first-rate player, although she is just two years older than Andrea. Andrea would like to follow in Tracy's winning footsteps. Odds are she will.